DIGITAL PRESENTATIONS

PHILADELPHIA PRESS

Philadelphia Press is an eco-friendly, environmentally conscious company. We strive to keep our carbon footprint to an absolute minimum, and to deliver non-paper products whenever possible.

All rights reserved. No part of this book may be reproduced or utilized in any form or by any means, electronic or mechanical, including photocopying and recording, or by any information storage and retrieval system without written permission from the publisher.
Copyright 2021
Books may be purchased for educational purposes.
For information, please call or write: (888) 851-3367
ISBN: 978-1-956331-00-4
Philadelphia Press
7715 Crittenden St. #390 • Philadelphia, PA 19118
Web site: wwwphiladelphiapress.com • Email: info@philadelphiapress.com

Printed in the United States of America

Contents

1 Introduction — 1
- What is a Virtual Presentation — 4
- The Communication Process — 5
- Benefits and Barriers of Virtual Presentations — 7
- When is Virtual the Preferred Option — 9
- Why Virtual Presentations Fail — 9

2 Face to Face versus Virtual Presentations — 13
- Commonalities — 13
- Differences Between Face-to-Face and Virtual Presentations — 21
- Effective Listening — 23
- Listening versus Hearing — 23

3 Analyzing the Audience — 29
- What Does Being Audience Centered Mean? — 30
- Different Types of Audiences — 34
- Situational Audience Analysis — 35
- Speaker Adaptation with Specific Audiences — 37
- Verbal Communication and the Effect on Audiences — 38
- Nonverbal Communication and the Effect on Audiences — 40
- Selecting an Audience Centered Topic — 41
- Speaker Challenges with Audiences — 42
- Strategies to Improve Speaker Dialogue with Diverse Audiences in Digital Presentations — 43

4 Finding Information Online — 51
- Gathering Information — 52
- Assessing Information — 58
- Placing Information — 65

5 Planning and Organizing — 69
- Planning and Outlining — 69
- How to Make an Outline — 71
- Introduction — 73
- Conclusions — 77
- Organizational Patterns — 80

⑥ Connecting With Your Audience Emotionally — 85

Using Emotion 85
Understanding the Emotions of Your Audience 86
Consider These Two Scenarios 87
How Can You Evoke Emotion in Your Audience 89
Using the Four Basic Emotions 90
What is Monroe's Motivated Sequence? 92
Using Language to Evoke Emotion 92
Using Emotion to Make an Argument 97
Arguments About Policy Change 100

⑦ Ethics in Online Communication — 105

Considering the ethics of Online Communication 105
NCA Credo for Ethical Communication 105
The Practice of Ethics in the Digital World 108
Types of Plagiarism 109
Respect Your Audience 114

⑧ Delivery of Online Communication — 123

Appearance 123
Background 126
Location 127
Nonverbal Communication 128
Paralanguage 131
Deliberating on Delivery for Online Communication 133

⑨ Anxiety and Apprehension for Online Communication — 135

Glossophobia, Social Phobia and Social Anxiety Disorder 135
Anxiety in a Digital World 137
The Betrayal and benefit of Biology 137
Managing Communication Apprehension 140

⑩ Visual Aids for Virtual Presentations — 149

Types of Visual Aids 150
Presentation Preparation 150
Visual Dos and Don'ts 153
Using Visual Aids in the Business World 155
Considerations of Visual Design 158
Four Golden Rules of Presentations 160
Wrapping it All Up 161

⑪ Virtual Meetings — 165

- Four Types of Virtual Meetings 165
- Planning a Virtual Meeting 166
- Assign Roles and Responsibilities 171
- Designing and Creating Presentations 172
- Conduct the Meeting: Day of Event 173
- Follow-Up 174
- Etiquette Tips for Participants 175

⑫ Moderating Virtual Panels and Presentations — 179

- Moderating a Panel 180
- Moderator Checklist 187
- What if You're a Panelist 188

⑬ Online Interviewing in a Post-Pandemic World — 193

- Types of Interviews 194
- Research and Practice 198
- Organized and Specific Responses 204
- Asking Questions Back 206
- What They See and Hear 207
- Post Interview Interaction 210
- Looking Back 211

Introduction

Allison S. Williams, EdD
Rowan University

In May of 1851, Sojourner Truth spoke at the Women's Rights' Convention in Akron, Ohio, delivering one of the most notable speeches in American history. Truth's words are known to have influenced both the women's rights and abolitionist movements, yet there is no verified transcript of what Truth presented since she gave the speech without written notes. In 1863, the woman who introduced Sojourner Truth to the Akron convention crowd twelve years prior, Frances Dana Gage, first published her account of Truth's speech in New York's The Independent. Gage's retelling heavily depicted Truth as having a southern dialect, though Truth was from the north, and included the now-famous reoccurring anaphora "Ar'n't I a woman?". Gage's version of Truth's speech was republished several times and became widely known.

Historians, however, note Gage's recollection is vastly different from an earlier account by Truth's trusted friend Marius Robinson, which was published in *The Anti-Slavery Bugle* the month following Truth's memorable delivery. The Sojourner Truth Project provides a side by side comparison of the two published versions. Although thematically similar, the varying lengths, different dialects, and Robinson's omission of any reference to the phrase, or a similarly worded version, of "Ain't I a Woman?" are startling. How could the two recollections be so vastly different? Where many historians support Robinson's version as likely more accurate due to his friendship with Truth, the lack of embellished dialect, and the timeliness of his publication, the fact remains that Truth's speech word-for-word will forever remain a mystery.

Today, it is unimaginable to believe a convention headliner's speech like Sojourner Truth's could be presented without accurate documentation. With modern technologies, the messages delivered by notable presenters and novice speakers alike can transcend time and distance through asynchronous and synchronous means. In the mid-nineteenth century and earlier, documenting oral presentations was limited to the accounts of in-person spectators and the speakers themselves. Still, the path to modern oratory preservation was underway less than ten years after Truth's 1851 speech.

In 1860, inventor Édouard-Léon Scott de Martinville captured the first-known recording of the human voice. Martinville's sound-capturing device, however, was unable to playback his recordings; therefore, the distinction of inventing the first device for audio recording and playback went to Thomas Edison, who developed the phonograph in 1877 (Fabry, 2018). Audio playback provided an asynchronous experience. Those unable to experience an auditory moment in real-time or those choosing to experience it again could hear the message after its recording.

Before the twentieth century, simultaneous or synchronous oral communication was limited to those in proximity to the speaker or those with wired telecommunication capabilities after Alexander Graham Bell's first U.S. telephone patent in 1876. Wireless communication was not far behind when in 1901, Guglielmo Marconi successfully sent and received radio signals across the Atlantic Ocean. Marconi's discovery that communication could successfully travel long distances via radio waves paved the way for new technology that would impact oral communication forever.

Before Marius Robinson's (1851) account of Sojourner Truth's speech, he wrote the following:

It is impossible to transfer it to paper or convey any adequate idea of the effect it produced upon the audience. Those only can appreciate it who saw her powerful form, her whole-souled earnest gestures and listened to her strong and truthful tones.

The technology boom of the twentieth century brought the ability for remote audiences to experience some of the effects Robinson refers to like never before. No longer did one need to be physically present in real-time to experience oratory history as it was happening. Historical moments played out over radio waves like the live broadcast of Franklin D. Roosevelt's December 8, 1941 address to Congress responding to the attack on Pearl Harbor. At the time, his speech "attracted the largest audience in radio history, with over 81 percent of all American homes tuning in" (Brown, 1998, p. 118). Roosevelt's paralanguage, which included his tone, elongated pauses, and inflection, communicated more than just his words as he opened with, "Yesterday, December 7, 1941, a date which will live in infamy."

The ability to communicate with both nonverbal and verbal means further expanded with television, permitting audiences to see body language, facial expressions, and gestures as they concurrently listened. On August 28, 1963, three major television networks in the United States, ABC, CBS, and NBC, aired Dr. Martin Luther King, Jr.'s "I Have a Dream" speech (Pruitt, 2021). Millions of television viewers, along with the approximately 250,000 in attendance at the National Mall in Washington, D.C., heard King's brilliant words and masterful use of vocalics. They saw his strength in posture and poise and experienced the magnitude of the repeated anaphora "Let freedom ring" as he held his hand up to the sky signaling "From every mountainside, let freedom ring."

Where radio and television broadcasts allow the speaker's message to reach the masses, unlike face-to-face communication, these technologies are linear or one-way, providing no means for immediate audience feedback. In the middle of the twentieth century, interactive audiovisual communication technology was developed with AT&T's picture-phone technology, but the systems and their successors were costly and problematic (Wolfe, 2019). However, the launch of the World Wide Web advanced videotelephony or videoconferencing capabilities, thus improving interactional, real-time, audiovisual communication. As web-enhanced personal devices became commonplace in the twenty-first century, audiovisual communication became more accessible for those with high-quality internet capacity. Virtual communication applications and platforms integrated audiovisual capabilities, providing useful tools to advance education, business, and personal communication. Before 2020, many people using audiovisual communication were doing so by choice.

Still, the COVID-19 global pandemic revolutionized the demand, as virtual communication technology provided the most similarities to face-to-face communication while accommodating the need for people to remain socially distant. Forced to navigate virtual communication platforms, many individuals persevered and successfully learned to use audiovisual, web-based tools, but how many did so with little thought of how the online medium impacted their ability to communicate effectively? Face-to-face and virtual communication share many commonalities, but the mediums' differences require careful consideration and the implementation of distinctive skills. Therefore, this textbook identifies the parallels of face-to-face and virtual communication while highlighting the unique skills essential for successful virtual presentation.

What is a Virtual Presentation?

The line "What's in a name? That which we call a rose by any other name would smell as sweet" from Shakespeare's *Romeo and Juliet* is a frequently used idiom meaning the names we assign objects, people, and concepts are not the objects, people, and concepts themselves. In other words, one should not be too invested in what something is called, and this is the case for virtual communication. As synchronous, audiovisual communication capabilities advanced, different terms were used to describe the technology. In some cases, the assigned labels were not completely accurate, leading to debate. For example, where many have accepted the term *virtual* to mean occurring online, the additional denotative meaning of the word is a simulation of something real. Since virtual communication is real, viable, and at times more feasible than face-to-face communication, some consider the term virtual to be misleading (Castaneda, 2018).

Other terms such as digital communication or online communication can also pose problems since these, along with virtual communication, can encompass a larger meaning than what is often intended. Suppose one wishes to specify a communicative activity that is synchronous with audiovisual capabilities. In that case, neither digital nor virtual nor online communication definitively describes the activity because all can include various forms of asynchronous exchange and verbal and nonverbal communication. With the various terminologies and interpretations, it is best to confirm all parties' expectations when planning virtual—or digital—or online communicative events. For this textbook, the terminology should be considered synonymous unless indicated otherwise. In addition, the following definitions for virtual events and virtual presentations will be used throughout this book:

INTRODUCTION

- According to *Meetings Today* (2012), "A virtual event is an occurrence of people gathering together where some or all of the attendees are not physically in the same location but are connected in a common environment."
- A virtual presentation is a smaller component or a larger virtual event (Marshall, 2021).

Considering these definitions, virtual presentations can take place for an array of occasions and for numerous reasons. Effective communication is key no matter the event or purpose; therefore, for a successful virtual presentation, one must understand the communication process.

The Communication Process

The communication process has several key aspects and while various models will contain slight variations, most consider the following as core components: the communicators, the exchange of meaning, the mode of delivery, the setting, and hindrances.

The Communicators

Some older communication models represent the communication process as linear or one-way. These models often indicate a sender as the sole communicator and fail to acknowledge the recipient's verbal and nonverbal feedback as an integral exchange of meaning. Modern models, however, acknowledge the exchange of information as ongoing and multidirectional. In a single communicative exchange, a communicator can take on the role of both the sender, the supplier of information, and the recipient, the one applying meaning to the information received.

The Exchange of Meaning

The exchange of meaning includes the message from the speaker or speakers and the feedback from the recipients. The information exchanged can be both verbal and nonverbal. Verbal information includes spoken, written, and nonverbal information, including meaning, derived without words through symbols such as images, body language, and paralanguage. In face-to-face public speaking situations, the recipient's or audience members' verbal responses are mostly limited to oral communication. Digital mediums, however, often provide features like chat functions or whiteboards, which permit opportunities for written feedback. And where nonverbal feedback is often easily accessible in face-to-face communication, digital settings require the recipients' use of video. They can be limited to how many video feeds are visible to the presenter or presenters.

The Mode of Delivery

The mode of delivery is often referred to as the channel or medium; it is the method used to deliver the exchange of meaning. Audiovisual communication is multimodal. Events, where some audience members are present face-to-face and others are virtual, are also multimodal. Even when there are multimodal channels available, there is no guarantee that all participants will engage using all available channels. For example, some online platforms allow users to connect with just audio; therefore, it is important to consider the intended mode of delivery from the participant's perspective. If someone intends to call in, a message dependent on a visual aid would not effectively communicate to that participant.

The Setting

Some communication process models omit the setting, which is also referred to as the *speaking situation*, but neglecting to consider the location and time of a presentation can be detrimental to its success. When choosing an ideal location, one must consider the following: available technology, potential distractions, set-up, and lighting. Time of day, week, month, and year can also impact one's approach to successful communication. With virtual presentations, these factors are considerably more complicated; participants' locations vary and, in some instances, like international presentations, time can too.

Hindrances

Hindrances, often referred to as *noise*, prevent the exchange of meaning because they disrupt the recipients' ability to apply meaning to the exchanged information. Where one immediately thinks of noise as being audible, hindrances come in many forms. They can be internal, unique to the recipient like a headache or worry, or external, contributing to the environment like overwhelming smells and extreme temperatures. A challenging aspect to virtual presenting is the potential for numerous hindrances to arise within the participants' locations. To address this challenge, virtual presenters should consider prevention methods designed to deter external hindrances from invading others' locations, like limiting who can mute and unmute their microphones. Since proactively managing hindrances can be a distraction itself, the presenters should consider assigning a presentation facilitator who is not scheduled to present. The facilitator can manage the audio and visual components and any other technical issues that may arise.

Benefits and Barriers of Virtual Presentations

When determining whether a presentation should be virtual or semi-virtual, one should take the time to consider the benefits and barriers. Common benefits to virtually presenting include the following:

* potential to save on expenses like venue and travel fees
* ability to reach a larger audience
* increased access to presenters and other resources not within proximity to the event
* reduced travel, which means more time for other tasks

Each benefit seems advantageous enough to determine virtual presenting as an ideal choice; one must also consider the potential barriers. These barriers include the following:

* adequate technology may not be available for all participants
* increased potential for technology issues
* increased potential for external hindrances
* reduced opportunity for nonverbal feedback
* increased opportunity for audience members to attempt to multitask, especially when others cannot see them checking emails or surfing the internet
* loss of participant-to-participant connections like friendly banter or chatting when sitting in a room face-to-face

How We Use Virtual Events

As a result of the Covid-19 pandemic, more people worldwide are aware of the many possibilities virtual communication platforms offer. The demand for virtual events will likely continue beyond pre-pandemic rates. According to Marshall (2021), virtual communication offers an array of possibilities, including the following and more:

Job Interviews	Key Account Meetings	Debating
Conferences & Conventions	Luncheons	Teaching
Fund-raising	Coaching	Networking
Casual Conversations	Selling Products	Cold Calls
Recruiting	Talking with Peers	Product Introductions
Board Meetings	Training	Q&A Sessions
Sales Meetings	Brainstorming Sessions	Updating Superiors
Team Presentations	Mentoring	Webinars

When is Virtual the Preferred Option?

The benefits and barriers will vary for every potential communicative activity and are influenced by factors such as the participants and their needs and the type of event and its purpose. In many instances, virtual or semi-virtual events are preferred when virtual presenting satisfies the need for interactive communication that is time-sensitive, cost-effective, and/or widespread. However, the criteria for deciding when virtual is the preferred option are not one-size-fits-all, and a simple nuance can determine whether virtual or semi-virtual is the right choice or if in-person is the better option. For example, imagine that a regional manager needs to set up a meeting for her district managers to learn about a new company policy. A virtual meeting will eliminate the need for the district managers to travel to one location; doing so will save the company money and prevent anyone from spending time away from their districts. If, however, one of the district managers is soon retiring after many years of services with the company, the regional manager may opt for a more costly in-person meeting to present the company's new policy as doing so also provides the opportunity for each district manager to provide their colleague a more personal and engaging farewell. In the latter scenario, although the primary purpose for the presentation could have been successfully accomplished with a virtual meeting, the regional manager's secondary goal of providing a retirement party for the district manager would have been less successful as a virtual event, especially if the gathering included a customary retirement cake. The desire to provide an engaging social experience can often lead one to choose face-to-face over virtual options. Still, in some cases, the in-person social element can thwart an event's success, especially if the agenda is fixed to a specific schedule, with the ability to control who can speak. Additionally, a virtual event may be a better choice when there is a need to limit the social aspect from overtaking a plan.

Why Virtual Presentations Fail

Inevitably, anyone regularly virtually presenting will experience a technology glitch or failure at some point. Knowing this, successful virtual presenters do not allow technology to dictate their ability to communicate effectively. If an intended video clip does not play, a successful speaker can summarize the video's message. If a panelist's audio stops working, a successful presentation organizer knows the agenda and substitutes it into the allotted spot until the problem is rectified. Technology issues may change a presentation's intended medium or require an altered message. Still, rarely should a technology problem halt the communication process entirely unless the issue is widespread, like power outages or network failures. Therefore, problems with technology, although inconvenient, are not why virtual presentations fail; they fail due to a lack of preparation.

The two key aspects of virtual presentation preparation are developing the message and considering the technology. Just like face-to-face presenting, preparing an effective message takes time and requires an audience and situational analyses, gathering research, message creation, and practicing the delivery. These aspects of message preparation are discussed in more detail in the chapters to come.

When considering the technology, one must consider the presenter or presenters' technology and the technology most likely used by the audience. When possible, presenters should always practice their delivery with the technology they plan to use during the presentation and take the opportunity to set preferred features to default. Imagine a virtual presenter holding up her company's new product to find the product name displayed backward and difficult to read. If this presenter had practiced with the presentation technology ahead of time, she would have discovered the issue. With a simple settings adjustment, the camera's mirror option could be turned off and be ready to capture text properly. When considering the audience's technology, those responsible for the presentation may need to communicate to the audience ahead of time to determine what technology the audience has available and how they plan to connect. For example, suppose the presentation occurs when audience members may need to log in on portable devices like smartphones or tablets. In that case, the presenter needs to remember that a visual successfully created on a 15-inch laptop does not present as effectively on a 6-inch smartphone. This textbook reminds presenters that technology should be considered part of the preparation process. It does not cover the types of virtual communication platforms and their available features. Technology is evolving quickly; therefore, it is a virtual presenter's responsibility to keep up to date and informed on technological advancements.

Conclusion

Technology not only ensures the documentation of modern speech; it allows oral communication to transcend time and distance. Digital technology has presented new forums for oral presentation. Where face-to-face and virtual events share some commonalities, the differences presented by the virtual medium require distinctive skills to ensure effective communication. Understanding virtual presenting, the characteristics that make it ideal or challenging, and effectively approaching virtual communication can make even a novice speaker a more confident and skilled digital presenter.

References

Brown, R. (1998). *Manipulating the ether: The power of broadcast radio in thirties America.* McFarland & Co.

Castaneda, D. (2018, December 31). *Let's distinguish online from virtual: It's time to stop calling all online interactions "virtual."* eLearning Industry. https://elearningindustry.com/distinguish-online-from-virtual-time-stop-calling-online-interactions-virtual

Fabry, M. (2018, May 1). *What was the first sound ever recorded by a machine?* TIME. https://time.com/5084599/first-recorded-sound/

Marshall, P. (2021, January 12). *Digital presentations: Introduction to course* [Lecture Recording]. Canvas@Rowan. https://online.rowan.edu/

Meetings Today (2012, August 20). *Virtual event definitions.* https://meetingstoday.com/articles/127174/virtual-event definitions#:~:text=Everything%20below%E2%80%A6and%20maybe%20more,connected%20in%20a%20common%20environment.

Pruitt, S. (2021, January 13). *7 things you may have not known about MLK's 'I Have a Dream' speech.* History. https://www.history.com/news/i-have-a-dream-speech-mlk-facts

Robinson, M. (Ed.). (1851, June 21). Women's rights convention: Sojourner Truth. *The Anti-Slavery Bugle.* The Library of Congress. https://chroniclingamerica.loc.gov/lccn/sn83035487/1851-06-21/ed-1/seq-4/

Wolfe, E. (2019, May 1). *The history of video conferencing from 1870 to today.* Lifesize. https://www.lifesize.com/en/blog/history-of-video-conferencing/

Face-to-Face vs. Virtual Presentations

Thomas S. Wright, PhD, Temple University
Maxine Gesualdi, PhD, West Chester University

This chapter is not about how one mode is better than the other but, instead, to show their productive intersection and overlap. Most importantly, none of the three presentation modes is likely to dominate or disappear any time soon. In-person job presentations and conferences where people can gather and talk will remain popular, but the accessibility and convenience of virtual presentations, not to mention the cost saving of reduced travel, ensure continued use. This chapter covers the most important aspects of this productive comparison between face-to-face and virtual presentations to enrich our understanding of each.

Commonalities

This section covers some of the many similarities between the two modes of presentation to improve our understanding of each.

Audience

The most fundamental commonality between any mode of presentation is an audience. You may have a job interview in person or virtually where you interact with one or many people. A commencement address may be presented in front of a hundred people or broadcast and recorded to be viewed by thousands. No matter the purpose or the occasion, a presentation is for someone or some audience. The audience's presence or the possibility that your presentation will be viewed sets it apart from everyday conversations. Your audience's size, makeup, and disposition determine, among many things, the content, style, length, and delivery of your presentation.

Time Limits

A vital characteristic of any presentation is a specified or recommended time limit. Most professional presentations, whether they are face-to-face or virtual, have a specified time. For example, a conference paper presentation may be between eight and fifteen minutes. A persuasive speech in a public speaking class is usually six to nine minutes. On the longer end, a customer- training session may last four hours or more. In each case, the presenter should know and honor the time limit specified. In a debate, you may even be penalized for exceeding your allotted time, and no one wants to overstay their welcome in a job interview. Perhaps the only difference between in-person and virtual presentations is that the audience can turn you off in a virtual presentation.

Beginning, Middle, and End

As outlined by Aristotle in The Rhetoric, 2,500 years ago, presentations have an introduction, body, and conclusion. This organizational pattern is most apparent in traditional speeches, informative, persuasive, and ceremonial, and board meetings, teaching demonstrations, and sales meetings. The audience expects the presenter or team to provide an overview, a well- structured presentation of the information and visuals, and a conclusion that ties everything together. In each case, face-to-face or virtually, audiences expect an organized interaction with strategic repetition that allows them to follow along.

Expected or Anticipated Outcomes

A professionally oriented presenter enters every speaking situation with a notion in mind of what they want to achieve. That is, they have an expected or anticipated outcome. At a luncheon or networking event, that outcome may strengthen existing relationships or make new ones. At a product introduction, like the rollout of the newest iPhone, the speaker expects the audience to be both "wowed" and more knowledgeable about the phone. A prevalent type of presentation is to update superiors on a project, evaluation, or sales meeting. The outcome, whether you are in the same room or on separate continents, had better be more informed and up- to-date bosses!

Planning

There are few times in professional life when you should have to "wing it" or give an impromptu presentation. Most presentations are planned, if not well in advance, then with enough time for you to consider what you will say, how you will say it, what visuals you want to use, and the primary audience. Even in situations in which you are unsure of specifically, who you may be addressing, for example, a job interview or networking event, you know the purpose of the interaction, and the person's work and organizational history. On the other end of the spectrum, a team sales presentation, you may know the date of your presentation days or even weeks in advance. Whether your team is in the conference room at the local Marriott or everyone is joining from their home office, your presentation should be a choreographed affair.

Visual Aids

Visual aids have become increasingly critical in every type and mode of presentation.

While some face-to-face interactions do not lend themselves to visual aids, such as a networking event or speed interviews, they are expected in most situations. We have become a more visually oriented society, and we now recognize that some people are visual learners. That is, they remember and process information more consistently when given visual cues to follow. First and foremost, they engage the audience and provide structure. You can show the audience the main points of your presentation or outline the flow of information. In some cases, due to the length of the presentation, such as training or seminar, it is bordering on unprofessional and certainly unproductive not to use visual aids to help with explanation and retention.

Preparation

Professional presentations take preparation. You or your team need to research or reach out to people to put together materials. If you are working in a team, you may need to meet several times or interact via Slack over the days or weeks beforehand. You have to collect, curate, tweak and organize your visual aids and add animations. You may have to research the audience to know who will be in attendance, what expectations they have for the event, and what questions they may ask. Preparation for face-to-face or virtual speeches differs, but many elements are precisely the same. You consider the problem, the pathway to resolving it, and meeting expectations, practicing, and presenting.

Rehearsal

Professional presentations require rehearsing your presentation. The content, length, and audience for your presentation may determine how much rehearsal you need. Relatedly, your familiarity with the material or topic may impact your rehearsal time. While there may be some minor differences in your approach, virtual and face-to-face presentations are more likely to be successful when you rehearse in conditions that mimic the setting or location for your presentation as closely as possible. In each case, you will review your notes and visual aids, time yourself, make adjustments to your delivery and rate, record yourself if possible, and become comfortable with your presentation's flow and language.

Delivery

Many of the essential elements of engaging the audience and making a professional delivery are the same for virtual and in-person presentations. These include eye contact, gestures, and facial expression. In each instance, the vocal characteristics of your delivery are paramount. These include vocal variety in pitch, cadence, inflection, rate, articulation, and reducing fillers (e.g., um, ah, "you know"). You are evaluated as credible during job interviews and organizational meetings based not only on what you know but how you perform the role. Additionally, how you present your visual aids and emphasize transitions is essential when you are in front of an audience, or they are watching on their phone. Your goal is to engage the audience, indicate which information is most important, and meet the occasion's delivery expectations.

Follow-up

Audience interaction is often the highlight of any presentation. After face-to-face and virtual presentations, depending on the presentation's purpose, the audience may have the opportunity to ask follow-up questions. Their questions may focus on clarifying information, making inquiries regarding additional information or seeking guidance. There may be challenges to persuasive appeals or people expanding on their own experiences. In an interview, there may be a continuous back and forth. The best approach is often to let the audience or those in attendance know that you welcome feedback and follow-up questions and have allotted time to do so.

Purpose

A relevant and enduring commonality between in-person and virtual presentations is that they have a purpose. In every case, the purpose of the event or interaction guides your preparation. It sets the stage for you and your audience and helps you determine what you or your organization wants to accomplish.

Purpose Guides Preparation

The most common purposes for presentations are to inform, persuade, or commemorate. An example of an informative presentation delivered in person or via Zoom is diversity training. In each instance, you educate and interact with the audience to help them make informed and ethical choices about their organization. An example of a persuasive presentation is for recruiting. Meeting with prospective students in person is sometimes convenient and practical, but in other instances, due to travel time and distance, they may opt to take a virtual campus visit. Ceremonial presentations have become hybrid events that allow the audience to participate in person or send their regards from all corners of the world. You don't have to limit your examples to traditional speeches. You prepare for job interviews by researching the organization and answering potential questions since your purpose is to get hired or get an internship.

Setting the Stage

Knowing the purpose of your presentation or interaction allows you to "set the stage" for the audience. For example, in virtual and face-to-face presentations, we can prepare the audience at the outset for your presentation's tone, upbeat or solemn, using an attention-getter. If your purpose is to inform the audience of the Black Lives Matter movement's history, you might set the stage with a somber recitation of names of black citizens who have died in police custody. If your purpose is to celebrate famous women who have graduated from your school, you might set the stage with an upbeat, inspirational story. If your purpose is to educate a professional audience in a training session or seminar, brevity and specificity guide how you prepare the audience to receive information.

Determine Your Goals

Ultimately, in-person and virtual presentations are driven by the goals of the speaker and the audience. Some common goals are educating the audience, convincing them to adopt a new product, informing them about organizational policy changes, or finding new contact persons via networking. Your planning and preparation should include audience analysis, even a cursory web search, or reaching out to a trusted contact person to ensure that you have a clear idea of the audience's expectations. While there does not need to be a perfect correlation between your goals and theirs, you can't succeed without understanding their perspective. If your goal or the ultimate purpose of your presentation can not meet their expectations, you may need to adjust or reconsider your purpose.

Expected Outcomes

Another commonality between virtual and face-to-face presentations is that their expected outcome drives your preparation and interaction with the audience. Some typical outcomes for presentations include moving the audience to do something, acquire a skill or knowledge, or start a conversation. No matter the expected outcome, you have to plan your presentation with that result in mind.

To-Do Something

One type of expected outcome is to have the audience do something. These types of presentations, either face-to-face or virtual, focus on practical changes a person or organization can make to add to or improve a product or procedure.

Change a Procedure

In any organization, procedural changes are routine and need to be communicated to members. For example, suppose your company is updating its procedures for handling customer inquiries. In that case, everyone on teams needs to know what the changes are, how those changes will impact outcomes, and who is in charge of implementing the new procedure. Likewise, a coach may have a new approach to practicing for the season or week. Face-to-face and virtual presentations ensure everyone understands a new or updated procedure. If you are the presenter covering the change of procedure, your most important task is to ensure everyone understands how the new procedure differs from the current one and why it is crucial.

Upgrade a Product

Information regarding upgrading a product is another common type of presentation. These presentations may be from an external vendor, either for sales, to explain a new version of the software or internally after the upgrade is purchased. It is essential to demonstrate the new product for potential clients, with the expected outcome being a sale or contact from a sales perspective.

Internally, rather than leave it to individual members to "figure it out," management may want to introduce the staff's software. Hence, everyone understands the purpose of the change and how it will affect their work. Suppose you are the presenter and want to propose a new product or an upgrade. In that case, your most important task is to ensure everyone understands the need for the new product and how it will improve the organization or their situation.

Update or Change a Policy

Policy changes are one of the most common types of corporate presentations. Some examples include changes to sick leave, attendance, accounting practices, meeting times, annual reviews, and food in the refrigerator. Since these impact the day-to-day work of organizational members and the quality of work time, they are important to communicate and discuss. Face-to-face and virtual presentations offer the opportunity to review the new policies and take questions about the changes. If you are the presenter updating the policy change, your most important task is to ensure everyone understands the new policy and how to comply.

To Acquire a Skill or Knowledge

Acquiring a new skill may take place in an organization or as part of your personal growth. You can learn how to play the drums with your teacher in the room or using your laptop. One of the amazing changes that have accompanied the growth of virtual interactions is our ability to learn a new skill with someone in the room or thousands of miles away. Similarly, for businesses, access to high-quality interactive training either onsite or virtually is a must. Some software and hardware's complexity requires a skilled teacher or trainer to communicate using visuals while also taking questions. If you are the lead person, your most important task is to ensure that everyone understands why the skill is necessary to the organization's continued success and growth.

Equally important is the acquisition of new knowledge, an integral part of your professional and personal growth. Professionally, you are constantly striving to understand better not only the organization you work for but also our "information environment." You should constantly be reviewing what is happening outside of the organization, from new competitors, to changes in government oversight, or potential new clients, to help them make informed choices. In face-to-face meetings and virtual conferences, you can gather the knowledge you need to succeed. You may also need to attend professional conventions to see the latest products, acquire new skills, and interact with colleagues. While it is always fun to attend in-person, virtual conferences or hybrids offer you the opportunity for professional growth. On the other hand, if you are presenting new information or knowledge, your primary goal is to ensure everyone understands and can take that knowledge with them.

To Start a Conversation

One of the great joys of life is meeting and interacting with people. You may engage in community outreach for your company, a candidate, or your social organization. The most fundamental aspect of that task is starting a conversation with people in the community. While face-to-face encounters are beneficial, the ability to have an "open door" or online listening session allows for working parents, persons with a disability, or someone struggling with a healthcare issue to join the conversation and be heard. Your conversations may deal with a specific public policy or the best way for your organization to set up a town hall. In each case, your central goal is to bring people into the conversation and encourage dialogue.

Starting a conversation may also serve a more professionally functional purpose. Networking and job interviews allow us to meet people who share our interests or help us advance in our field. The growth of networking, interacting with others to gain information, or create social and professional contacts, is encouraged and expected in many fields. Since you may change jobs many times during your career, building an extensive network of contacts is advantageous. Your central goal when starting a conversation is not to exploit the goodwill of others but to enter into a mutually beneficial professional relationship.

Differences Between Face-to-Face and Virtual Presentations

Let's face it, virtual presentations are here to stay. The flexibility and savings associated with virtual presentations mean organizations now have options when connecting with their audiences. As already noted, virtual presentations come with some benefits over face-to-face presentations. Still, to fully appreciate virtual presentations, discussing some of the key differences between them is productive.

Potential Distractions

You are in a shared physical space in the ideal presentation situation, interacting with your audience. Since the audience is often seated or standing facing you, the audience's attention is continuously directed toward you. The audience is facing you the entire time. So, while there may be distractions, you, as the speaker, have an unusual amount of control. You may have heard the phrase "captive audience," which means the audience must pay attention because of the presentation context.

When making a virtual presentation, however, you compete with many potential distractions. These distractions are not the audience's fault but, rather, the context of the presentation. Your audience may be in an open-work space using earbuds. Perhaps they are in their car. They may be in their home office or sitting on their deck. We all have had to compete for attention from coworkers, deliveries, children, pets, technical problems, phones, and the internet. Our approach is to accept these as a natural part of the presentation process and not blame the audience. If we accept that distractions will happen, we can better prepare our presentations to meet the situation.

Less Physical Performance

The most significant difference between in-person and virtual presentations is that you are not sharing the same physical space. When planning and making virtual presentations, you depend less on the more conventional and formal aspects of physical performance. You do not have at your disposal the taken-for-granted tools of gesture and comportment, roving eye contact, and changing your posture. While some virtual presentations are given while standing, either on a stage or using a green screen, the most common setting is

the presenter sitting down in front of a camera. Virtual presentations are considerably more static and stationary than in-person presentations. Because you are using a tablet, desktop camera, or laptop, you must square your shoulders, look directly into the camera, and move as little as possible to stay in the frame.

Speaking Takes Center Stage

Since your physical performance space is reduced considerably during virtual presentations, speaking and facial cues take center stage. Virtual presentations ask us to use the entire dynamic range of our voices. While the content of your presentations will most likely be professionally oriented, the best approach is to treat virtual presentations like talking to a friend. When you talk to a friend, you will notice, your voice is very expressive. You adjust the tone, rate, pitch, and volume to make a point, bring a story to life, and get a reaction. Your voice is used to direct attention, provide emphasis, and engage the audience.

Similarly, your facial expressions and paralinguistic cues take on a special emphasis when on camera. Even if you are screen sharing, the audience is drawn toward the action, your facial expressions, and cues. Although you are not making direct eye contact, your eyes, squinting or wide open, looking directly into the camera or focused elsewhere, provide a natural indication of how you feel and how the audience should understand the information presented.

Emphasize Engagement

Since your virtual presentation is in competition with potential distractions, and your delivery repertoire is more limited, it is necessary to emphasize audience engagement. In some ways, your approach in the virtual environment is not different from face-to-face interaction. You always want the audience to be attentive and engaged, reacting, asking questions, and providing nonverbal feedback. It is helpful when you use all the common interpersonal and technological tools available to drive the feedback loop in a virtual environment. It is helpful to let the audience know at the outset whether you will be taking questions, spoken or in a chat feed and when you will address those questions. You should encourage attendees to raise their digital "hand" or use other icons to get your attention. Finally, virtual fatigue is real. Everyone gets tired after looking at a screen all day. To foster engagement and maintain attention, you can build in surveys, give the audience a short break, and ask for comments and questions when they return, or have all of them share their screen.

Effective Listening

Effective listening is one of the least discussed and most important aspects of communication. It is often taken for granted that everyone is born with the skill of listening productively and with intention. As in other presentation situations, keeping the audience listening and attentive is key to a successful virtual interaction. This section will discuss the difference between listening and hearing, encouraging active listening, and the enemies of effective listening, distractions, and multi-tasking, respectively.

Listening versus Hearing

A pervasive misperception is that hearing is listening. However, it is not usual to hear background chatter before a virtual presentation. For example, your coworkers are catching up on their weekend plans and discussing the projects due this week. You can hear them, but you are not listening to the content of their interactions. A meaningful way to frame your understanding of presentations is to consider the context in which the audience receives your message. As a presenter, you compete with distractions that are out of your control—this not the fault of the audience but, rather, a product of the circumstances. However, as we will discuss, know that listening takes effort, and your audience is disadvantaged compared to a face-to-face meeting, which means you may need to make some adjustments.

Hearing is Passive

Hearing is a passive act. As described in the example above, we hear many different conversations and sounds that intrude into our environment but cannot remember them later or even recall they were present. That is because we did not attend to them. We did not call them out of the background and listen to them to process or remember them. Quick experiment. What was the second sound you heard this morning? The first was probably your alarm, but what was the second? It had to be something, right. You heard it, but you did not listen to it. Presentations, especially virtual presentations, require the speaker to create an atmosphere that encourages active listening.

Listening is a Conscious Choice

Listening is primarily a conscious choice. You choose to pay attention to, process and reflect on the messages you receive from a friend, salespersons, television shows, and during a presentation. While sounds or stimuli may initially grab our attention, like a loud sound at the start of a commercial or compelling introductory video before a speech, without choosing to listen further, listening fades to merely hearing quickly. During a virtual tour of campus, you must purposefully act to maintain the processing of the information provided. As a speaker, since we know listening is a conscious choice, your goal is to provide a compelling reason to keep listening, using all your delivery tools. These tools include your voice, engaging content, and visual cues that require the audience's attention and make it worth their while.

Listening Requires Energy and Motivation

Since listening is an involved activity, it takes energy and motivation. Even the most seasoned and skilled participant will feel their attention wane at times. Waning attention occurs because listening, the act of engaging and processing messages, uses mental energy. And different types of presentations, face-to-face and virtual, will require different amounts of energy, depending on the content of the presentation and our knowledge of the material. For example, lectures, seminars, training sessions, and debates often call for us to pay close attention to specific processes and pieces of information. A good presenter knows this and takes it into account by providing physical and mental breaks, visual cues, and the strategic use of repetition.

On the other hand, if you are more familiar with the content of a presentation, you can use less active listening. Relatedly, listening takes motivation. While you are the presenter, you are not responsible for everyone's level of motivation. However, you are responsible for crafting a presentation that gives the audience a reason to maintain active listening.

Encouraging Active Listening

Although you cannot control any audience's level of motivation, you can create an environment that encourages and rewards active listening. One of the most fruitful approaches is to begin by taking the audience's perspective, which is not just an audience analysis of who will be in the audience but considering how they encounter your presentation. How many boring virtual presentations have you sat through? And what is a common problem? The presenter is only focused on an information dump--getting out as much information as quickly as possible.

To that end, like any good presentation, a virtual presentation should be well organized (meandering and off-topic leads to hearing, not listening), provide compelling content (information, knowledge, or perspective that benefits the listener), and use a dynamic style of delivery appropriate to the occasion (nothing leads to loss of hearing faster than someone not worth listening to).

Additionally, encourage your audience to take handwritten notes. It may seem counter-intuitive but active listening is often attained by concentrating and transcribing key points, questions, and comments. Jotting these down allows the audience to bring more to the discussion than their remembrances. Handwritten notes free up our memories and minds to process the content of presentations and offer considered responses.

Distractions Impact Effective Listening

As you now know, effective listening is not a passive exercise but a conscious choice that takes energy and motivation and some help from engaging presenters. Unfortunately, what makes active listening even more challenging are pervasive distractions in the audience's environment and the myth of multi-tasking. Each of these is an enemy of effective listening.

They sabotage not only our best efforts at creating a dynamic and engaging experience but rob audience members of their attention and understanding of the material. In addition, they steal energy, disrupt concentration and recall, and affect other participants' perceptions.

In a virtual environment, distractions are inevitable for the presenter and the audience. As a presenter, you generally have more control over the situation, and you should have already prepared for possible diversions. Like a face-to-face presentation, knowing your environment and practicing will eliminate many possible issues. More importantly, just as impactful are distractions that keep the audience from effectively listening. While you cannot control where an audience receives your message, knowing the challenges they face allows you to prepare better by using memorable visuals, breaks, repetition, and shared materials. So, what are some potential distractions?

External distraction

External distractions include anything in the audience's field of view, including noise outside or inside their environment and conversations. For example, although it is nice to have a view when a bird appears or a crash happens, some audience members may lose focus. Similarly, a persistent distraction in the workplace includes coworkers "dropping in," the continuous need to answer emails and DMs, and tabs in the browser. What is this? Physical discomfort is another form of external distraction. Someone may be hot or cold, it may be windy, or their chair is hard to sit in. It is always important to remind your audience to mute their microphone, so their distractions don't become everyone's distractions.

Internal distraction

Internal distractions are even more difficult to address than external distractions since they are something the audience is experiencing mentally. These distractions can include worry, emotional turmoil, or problems paying attention. If you experience a distraction, it may be evident to the audience and require a brief explanation. On the other hand, it may be hard to know the audience's mental state unless it is obvious. For example, everyone has dealt with a sick child or family member, concern over a work project, and the stress over meeting a deadline. Since these factors are out of your control, your best approach is to provide an engaging experience that uses visual cues and repetition that makes your material easier to remember.

The Multi-Tasking Myth

Another perhaps unlikely distraction that prevents the audience from engaging in effective listening is multi-tasking. Multi-tasking is when a person attempts to complete one or more cognitive tasks, seemingly simultaneously. An example of multi-tasking in the workplace is working on a design project simultaneously as DMing, a coworker while taking a phone call.

While the phrase is a part of contemporary culture, multi-tasking is impossible because the human brain cannot attend to and complete multiple tasks simultaneously. While people believe they are efficient, they are doing many tasks poorly. Your brain switches back and forth between tasks rather than focusing on doing one task correctly. You can have many tasks to complete at your fingertips but quickly dancing between different ones is ineffective. The myth is especially pronounced in regards to listening. Active, effective listening, as previously discussed, is not possible when we are typing messages, reviewing written work, watching videos, or editing slides. As a presenter, you cannot keep people in a virtual environment from attending to other stimuli. However, by using many of the techniques discussed in this chapter and those that follow, you can create a situation where the audience needs to pay attention and listen closely.

Conclusion

In this chapter, we identified the commonalities between face-to-face and virtual presentations, including the time limits, organization, outcomes, planning, rehearsal, and the use of visual aids. Next, we explained how the purpose of a presentation guides its creation. We also described the expected outcomes for face-to-face and virtual presentations. These outcomes include doing something (for example, upgrading a product), acquiring knowledge (for example, training), and starting a conversation. Additionally, we discussed the differences between face-to- face and virtual presentations. Some differences include potential distractions, less physical and more vocal performance, and a heightened level of engagement. Finally, we outlined the importance of effective listening, noting how it is distinct from hearing. Knowing that your audience may face challenges to effective listening, it is helpful to use specific techniques to keep them engaged.

Analyzing the Audience

David M. Pallant
County College of Morris

Preface:

My experience as an educator/scholar, husband/father/brother, student of political communication, and community/union organizer has led me down many paths. Still, one thing is constant when presenting, strategic communication is learned, first by listening and then by practicing. Historically, great communicators have some common traits, whether in politics, business, or work/home environments. Great communicators employ empathy for an audience and have credibility and authenticity. As digital presenters we must employ various techniques to draw an audience into the speakers' worldview.

Aristotle, in his *Rhetoric,* said it best when he spoke of "An emotional speaker always makes his audience feel with him, even when there is nothing in his arguments; which is why many speakers try to overwhelm their audience by mere noise."

Of the modes of persuasion furnished by the spoken word, there are three kinds. The first kind depends on the personal character of the speaker; the second on putting the audience into a certain frame of mind; the third on the proof, provided by the words of the speech itself" (Aristotle, *Rhetoric*).

Please review these two examples and consider how the speakers motivate and persuade an audience to join their cause.

- How did they put the audience into a certain frame of mind?
- Why was the speakers' analysis of a live audience so important to their success?
- What verbal or nonverbal communication techniques did the speakers employ to engage the audience?
- How did the speakers' cadence or rhythm of speaking coach the audience to their perspective?
- How will your audience differ from these two examples in your digital presentations for this course?

What Does Being Audience Centered Mean?

Audience analysis is one of the most important parts of your speech. An audience can transform your speech positively or negatively. However, the speaker can transform an audience through powerful stories, proper verbal communication, and appropriate nonverbal communication cues. Yet, in virtual contexts, the challenge of engaging audiences can be quite different than in non-mediated. Mediated communication is when a medium is used to communicate. Computer-assisted or interpersonal mediated communication is what you will be doing during your digital presentations. A virtual speaker must plan and almost manufacture audience engagement by setting the stage for the performance. This chapter will show how a well-organized presentation on a video platform, considers who the audience is, their expectations, their potential distractions, and what goals you as a digital speaker have for audience participation.

You may now wonder what an audience is? As defined by dictionary.com, an audience is:

- the group of spectators at a public event, listeners or viewers collectively, as in attendance at a theater or concert,
- The opportunity to be heard; a chance to speak to or before a person or group; a hearing.
- the act of hearing, or attending to, words or sounds (http://www.dictionary.com/browse/audience).

The successful speaker should dedicate a large portion of time to audience analysis and topic selection. Digital speakers have a responsibility to consider the powerful relationship between the speaker and the audience. The audience sees, hears, and follows the command of the speaker. You guide the audience and have a unique role in creating a specific message and assisting the audience in their comprehension and retention of the message. Being audience-centered involves demographic research, self-reflection, and adaptation.

How Does an Online/Virtual Speech Differ from a Face-Face Speech?

When presented with an online speech, one must first ask a few important questions about the audience:

- Why am I speaking to this audience? In the online context you could be speaking for a digital presentation assignment in class, interview for employment, or corporate training, or sales pitch for a corporation.
- Who specifically is in my audience? An online speech could be a much larger audience with more diverse needs.
- What are the motivations or expectations of the audience? Online audiences may sit silent or ask many more questions.
- In what context is this speech being made?
- In what environment or location will I be speaking?
- How is the topic I choose audience-centered?
- Will the speech be synchronous or asynchronous communication?
- Synchronous communication is when communication takes place live and in real time with an audience.
- Asynchronous communication is when communication has been previously recorded or occurs at the individual's own time or has a lag in time.
- What are the limitations of online communication or of the specific platform that I will be using?

Likely, the answer to the first question of **"Why am I speaking to this audience?"** is that I am required to take this digital presentations course as part of my major requirement. However, various types of speeches require different approaches toward the audience. For example, an **informative speech** seeks to provide clear and concise information in a logical order to educate the audience. A **persuasive speech** employs communication strategies to motivate the audience toward a certain point of view. An **entertainment**

speech uses both techniques to educate and motivate an audience. However, all successful digital presentations incorporate the speaker's storytelling ability and connection with diverse audiences through powerful image-making.

Being an audience-centered speaker, we then ask, "Who specifically is in my audience?" The audience may consist of many different types of people, and it is important to gain knowledge about these people using formal or informal methods. The *demographics* of the audience are the unique characteristics and identities of the individuals. We have all taken surveys for employment or marketing purposes, and these types of surveys are formal primary research methods for demographic and product research. If you do have the time and opportunity to ask formal survey questions through Survey Monkey, for example, this will aid in accessing the audience's knowledge of the subject of the speech. You may want to collect some information from the audience before the day of the speech. A simple survey including questions on the speech topic and audience demographics would assist the speaker in tailoring the speech to the audience's needs and wants.

However, digital speakers do not always get an opportunity to deploy a formal survey to an audience before delivering a speech. Thus, it would be important to do some secondary research on who the audience is, what previous knowledge they have of the speech subject, and from this information develop the best approaches to successful audience-centered speaking. For example, before presenting to the audience, why not consider the diversity of the audience. Consider the education level, socio-cultural, socio-economic, gender, race, and sexual orientation as elements of diverse audiences. Remember, the individual audience members listening to a speech bring certain expectations and can assist the speaker by active listening and giving appropriate feedback.

What are the motivations and expectations of the audience? Each audience member brings pre-existing notions and experiences to each speech. The three types of audience motivations that are important to remember when preparing and delivering a digital speech are **attitudes, beliefs,** *and* **values.** The *audience's attitude* is simply a liking or disliking of something or someone. The *audience's belief* is an idea about what is true or false. *Audience values* are deeply held personal judgments about what is right or wrong. Remember that audience attitudes can change daily or even hourly. Audience attitudes are the easiest elements to change during a speech, followed by the audience's beliefs. Lastly, audience values are rarely changed during a single speech due to the long-term audience development of right and wrong.

In what **context** *is this speech being made?* The speech context refers to the occasion or historical time. Context matters to audiences because it can change how they receive the speech. Part of the context is the use of the speaker's verbal and nonverbal communication and also the events that surround the speech. For example, a speech presented on terrorism before September 11th versus a speech given after September 11th has a very different context. Or, as another example, a digital speech delivered on a video platform before the Covid 19 pandemic versus during the pandemic has a very different context. Audiences would expect a speaker to adapt the speech to the new context, and here is where context matters in developing a successful speech.

The wedding speech is a certain context or occasion. It infers that you will be considerate of the audience and not share too much information to embarrass or denigrate a dear friend or family member. The context is important to consider because you will need to provide personal stories and tribute to a close family member or friend, all while adapting your delivery to a diverse and, many times, unknown audience. Realizing that most of your audience has been on platforms for work or school for well over a year during a pandemic, you must realize that there is a sort of "Zoom fatigue" or natural inclination for audiences to tune out. To avoid these distractions it is a good idea to spend time on the use of your voice in digital presentations, incorporate audience exercises like short questions that peak or summarize information, and consider how your background visuals can enhance audience apprehension.

In what **environment** *or location will I be speaking?* Where a speaker presents the speech is the known environment or location of the speech, which could include numerous settings such as a classroom, video systems like Zoom, WebEx, or Shindig, an auditorium, outdoors, and a conference room. Certain environments for speeches require careful considerations. For example, if the audience is too large and your speech is scheduled for outdoors, you may want to consider amplification through a microphone or video screens to assist the audience in hearing and seeing the presentation. If the speech is being delivered in a large lecture hall that holds one hundred students, but your class only has twenty students, you may ask the audience on the day of the speech to sit in the first three rows to improve the distance between the speaker and the audience. Asking an audience that only has audio engaged to engage their audio and video would be an important speaker request and improve audience participation. However, it may also feel like speaker pressure to put audience members on the spot, creating audience apprehension toward engagement.

How is the topic I choose audience centered? The initial brainstorming, research on the topic, and finally, selecting the topic are all important steps to a well-crafted speech. However, many different types of audiences and topics should be considered.

Different Types of Audiences

A speaker should consider various types of audiences when selecting a topic and delivering the speech. Among the types of audiences are the following:

- **Active Audience:** An active audience is engaged, enthusiastic, and works to listen effectively to the speaker and the speech.
- **Passive Audience:** A passive audience is physically present but not fully engaged in the speech. A passive audience can easily be distracted and tune out during the speech.
- **Captive Audience:** Members of audiences can consider themselves captive or forced to attend a speech or presentation. For example, a state-required workshop or training for employees could be a context where the audience feels captive due to organizational, legal obligations. The speaker must not view them as captives and find a way to show their value to the individuals in the room.
- **Supportive Audience:** A supportive audience might have built a relationship with the speaker or topic previously, and you are speaking to the choir.
- **Voluntary Audience:** The voluntary audience has offered to attend the speech or presentation because of personal interest or value.

- **Involuntary Audience:** The involuntary audience could be similar to the captive audience, but they have been chosen by someone else to attend a speech and may not be as difficult of an audience to deal with.
- **Hostile Audience:** A hostile audience arises for many different reasons, including previous failed attempts of the speaker to connect with the audience. A second reason audience members or speakers can become hostile is if they believe their opinions have been ignored or the speaker or audience has lost credibility. Lastly, audiences may have different goals than the speaker's intended message, which might create conflict. An example of a hostile audience would be a press secretary for the president speaking to reporters during a press conference.
- **Large or Small Audiences:** The size of an audience matters, and the greater number of audience members increases the chances for misinterpretation or lack of comprehension.

Situational Audience Analysis

When addressing audiences, we must consider the situation of the speech. Speakers should adapt to the **time, size, location,** and **occasion** of the digital speech. If we can take on the role of an audience member and be empathetic speakers, we can adapt our speaking style and delivery more successfully.

Time in the speech-making process includes the actual day, specific time, and length of time we will speak with our audience. The study of the use of time in nonverbal communication is called **chronemics**. Chronemic preferences can change the speakers or audiences depending on their cultural identity, power or control relationship, and time orientations.

For example, when scheduling an interview, you may be provided a few options to meet, some in the morning and some in the afternoon. A competent speaker must consider when the best time is to speak. Ask yourself, are you a morning person or an afternoon person? Decide which specific time you will be most effective with audience engagement and persuasion. The decisions to arrive early, on time, or late for the interview are decided by the time orientation of the culture. If, for instance, you are scheduled to present digitally to employees for a training workshop on Monday morning after a week-long break, it will be important to gain the audience's attention early on in the speech and empathize with the audience if they are distracted or passive.

If you deliver a speech for a digital presentations course, your professor will usually provide a time requirement for the assignment. The minimum and maximum time requirements will many times be a portion of your grade, and also is the only way to allow for all students the ability to present their speech on the assigned days. When practicing your online speech, make sure to time the entire speech with a stopwatch, and allow for the appropriate pacing, pauses, and potential audience feedback.

The second key aspect of situational audience analysis is the total **size** of your audience. Audiences vary not only in individual demographics but also in the total number of people. There are a few reasons that the larger the audience is, the more difficult it is to engage. First, speaker communication apprehension can increase when more individuals watch, listen, and judge the speaker. Secondly, the larger number of audience members can lead to misunderstanding and inaccurate message dissemination. Each audience member has a unique listening and speaking style and can influence other audience members to interpret the speech.

The smaller number of audience members can also present unique challenges. The digital presentation delivered to a small audience can potentially become too personal and be considered an informal conversation that does not accomplish the intended goals. Informal conversation has very different verbal and nonverbal communication than public speech. Audiences may be intimidated by the informal nature and have different expectations, and, in turn, create an awkward silence.

The third part of situational audience analysis is the **location** of the speech. Remember that all speeches are a form of public communication or public address. However, during a digital presentation a speech should be delivered with the notion that an audience will watch, listen, and react to it. Where a digital speech is delivered is not always the choice of the speaker, but speakers can work to improve the location or listening environment.

Lastly, the **occasion** or event speech can combine these speeches' general purposes to inform, entertain, persuade, or tell a story. Audiences have certain expectations for each of these speeches, and a speaker should consider the occasion of the speech. A eulogy speech is an important occasion, one that provides a tribute to a loved one and can assist the audience in mourning by incorporating powerful empathetic storytelling. A speech like this can employ humor and heal and motivate an audience to overcome their sadness; if it is delivered correctly, it can transform a solemn audience into one of hope.

Speaker Adaptation with Specific Audiences

In this section, we need to consider the power of a word or combination of words to inform, entertain, and persuade an audience. In informative speaking, a speaker needs to use descriptive language and statistics that educate the audience and consider the audience's level of knowledge on the topic. In narrative and entertaining speeches, a speaker needs to use language that elicits powerful images and stories that the audience can relate to. In persuasive speaking, a speaker needs to craft strategic messages that consider the audience's experiences, needs, wants, and fears. Persuasive speaking attempts to change the attitudes and opinions of the audience through the Aristotelian persuasive appeals of ethos, logos, and pathos.

The 2016 presidential campaign provided numerous examples of candidates allowing the audience to control the message by adapting language, phrases, and call-and-response chants. The language used during this campaign created a symbolic and authentic relationship with the audience. With further analysis, we can see how two candidates adjusted their language and speech content when crowds or audiences became unwieldy and irrational. The powerful use of audience-centered language, which we discuss next, profoundly affected the growth of these political campaigns and their crowds.

Predicting audience reaction to your digital speech may be difficult. Still, it is important to continue to adapt to your audience's reaction. As discussed previously, audiences present different challenges through their different sizes, types, and demographics. It is important to remember that audiences can help or harm your speech presentation. Speakers need to interpret verbal or nonverbal audience reactions into a positive aspect of the speech delivery in real-time.

Verbal Communication and the Effect on Audiences

Maya Angelou:
"Words are things, I am convinced
You must be careful, careful about the words you use
Or the words you allow to be used in your house.
In the Old Testament we are told in Genesis (actually it's John 1:1)
That in the beginning was the Word
And the Word was God and the Word was with God

That's in Genesis (John 1:1).
Words are things
You must be careful
Careful about calling people out of their names
Using racial pejoratives and sexual pejoratives
And all that ignorance
Don't do that.
Someday we'll be able to measure the power of words.
I think they are things.
I think they get on the walls, they get in your wallpaper, they get in your rugs
In your upholstery, in your clothes and finally...
Into you."

The words we choose to use during a digital presentation are important signifiers to the audience of our intended meanings. Words can inform, persuade, and entertain an audience. A carefully chosen word can be a powerful way to introduce an audience to our presentation or also to conclude the presentation. Audiences will react to words that stimulate knowledge in an informative speech or want to take action or actively pursue change in a persuasive speech.

When delivering a narrative or entertainment speech, it is important to empathize with the audience through the structures of the stories you present. Stories can have a powerful effect on audiences because they transport an audience to a certain personal experience or moment in their lives. Audiences many times connect with the content of a speech when proper narrative structure is implemented within the presentation. All stories have a background, actions, taking place in certain settings that transport audiences, with specific defined characters and a climax that resolves conflict and many times leaves an audience with a lesson or moral. Great stories are repetitive, which improves audience retention of the message. They use highly personal language and effectively use silence and pauses in the speech. In persuasive speaking, the appropriate use of language can challenge an audience to choose a side of an argument, adopt a policy, or a specific attitude.

However, sometimes words can have intended or unintended impacts on audiences. In an example from political communication and presidential policy framing, we see Vice President Al Gore used the words *Global Warming* during his *Inconvenient Truth* documentary. In response to Al Gore, George W. Bush's administration made sure to re-frame the term *Climate Change*. When President Barack Obama was elected, his administration changed it again to *Global Climate Disruption*. If we look at Global Warming, Gore was inferring that humans were to blame for the clear warming of the earth due to increased CO_2 levels. Bush's use of the term *Climate Change* tried to downplay the human impact but inferred that change is occurring, maybe by artificial or natural climate changes. Lastly, Obama's use of *Global Climate Disruption* was inferring climate change's destructive and global nature. This language inferred that the loss of life and habitat for humans and animals would occur, and economic destruction and geo-political changes would stem from climate-related natural disasters.

Words have the power to educate, persuade, and entertain. Speakers need to be conscious of how certain audiences may interpret specific words and always look to be sensitive to an audience's experiences and cultural identities.

Nonverbal Communication and the Effect on Audiences

> "[I]t is not enough to know what we ought to say; we must also say it as we ought ... It is, essentially, a matter of the right management of the voice to express the various emotions—of speaking loudly, softly, or between the two; of high, low, or intermediate pitch; of the various rhythms that suit various subjects. These are the three things—volume of sound, modulation of pitch, and rhythm—that a speaker bears in mind."
>
> — Aristotle

Let us now look at paralanguage or vocalics, which is an aspect of nonverbal communication. *Paralanguage* studies the speaker's tone, rate of speech, volume, and pitch during a speech. As Aristotle states, managing these aspects of a speaker's voice is as important as what we are saying. The nonverbal communication that audiences provide during a speech is just as important as verbal communication. The feedback of the audience should be considered and monitored throughout the speech delivery. Most formal speeches do not allow for feedback in the form of questions or clarifications during the speech; however, they may allow for questions at the end of the speech. In your digital presentations should you stand, sit in front of a desk or podium? Does the use of a podium assist or create a barrier with the audience? Most audiences would infer that when a speaker uses a podium that this will be a formal speech, with limited audience feedback, and audiences would expect formal verbal and nonverbal communication from the speaker. You may also choose to have audio only for a digital presentation.

A podium or a fixed microphone/desk may restrict the **Kinesics** of the speaker. . *Kinesics* is the study of the way that certain body movements and gestures are part of nonverbal communication. If you choose a certain position for your body during a digital presentation you should stay with it during the entire presentation. Constant changes can be distracting for audiences. Speakers can move furniture, adjust backlighting, ask an audience member to pay attention by putting on video but we should always attempt to reduce distractions for the audience.

An audience provides numerous signals to the speaker that they are paying attention, agreeing or disagreeing, or are confused with the content of the speech or the delivery style. Great speakers have a unique skill for discerning audience approval or rejection and can adapt to difficult audience situations. The obvious areas a speaker can pay attention to in the audience members are their eyes, head, posture, and overall attentiveness. If the speaker notices that the audience members are taking notes, showing approving head nods, maintaining eye contact, smiling, and providing positive gestures, then the speaker can infer that the speech is connecting with this audience. If the speaker notices that the audience is showing disapproving head nods, eye contact to others in the room, frowning and providing negative gestures, then the speaker will need to adjust or adapt the speech delivery to re-engage the audience. However, in digital presentations this task may be more difficult. A monitoring of a chat feature may be appropriate in order to provide the audience with clarifications or more information.

So the next question would be, how does a speaker re-engage an inattentive audience?

Here are a few recommendations:
- Ask a rhetorical question or direct question in the chat feature of the video platform to the audience to show that you are an audience-centered speaker.
- Tell a story. Choose to tell a story that somehow connects the content of the digital presentation to the audience's experiences, wants, or needs.
- Use self-disclosures to the audience so they can trust you or find ways to rebuild your credibility with this audience.
- Use humor or satire.
- Use an audio-video clip.
- Increase rate of speech or volume.

Selecting an Audience Centered Topic
Overall Questions to Consider when Selecting a Topic
- Who is the audience? (What are their demographics)?
- What are the needs of the audience? (Do they need information? Do they want to be entertained? Should they be persuaded to do something that might help them in some way?)
- What are the audience's expectations? (What rules are dictated by the context?)
- Why should the audience care about this topic?
- What are my goals in speaking to this audience?
- Will the audience be receptive or skeptical? Friendly or hostile?
- Will the audience be voluntary? Are they being incentivized in some way?
- What questions might come from the audience after my speech?

In addition, the topic you choose should be:
- Timely and relevant to the audience
- Based on research instead of "common sense"
- Well-established with credible sources
- Interesting and engaging to the audience
- Commensurate with the audience's level of knowledge on the subject
- Authentic: based on your own experiences, interests, and talents.

Speaker Challenges With Audiences

- **Credibility:** Digital presentations need to already have or establish credibility or trust with an audience. Audiences will not listen to a speaker who lacks credibility.
- **Self-Disclosure:** Each speech has a credibility statement; this is where the speakers share something about themselves. When speakers self-disclose with an audience, it can help connect the central idea of the speech with the audience. However, too much information or over disclosing can negatively impact an audience.

- **Polarization:** A speaker can push an audience toward a perspective by using extreme examples or language that may polarize the audience. A polarized audience can tune out the speaker or react negatively toward the speaker.
- **Misreading Expectations:** Audiences may have certain expectations based on previous encounters with the speaker, and a speaker may wrongly judge the dynamics of the audience, which creates a hostile audience.
- **Speaking Down to the Audience:** Speakers can incorrectly use their position of power as speakers and speak down to the audience, manifesting in condescending statements, awkward silence, audience inattentiveness, and improper use of language. Audiences can feel inferior when a speaker speaks down to them.
- **Ignoring Nonverbal and Verbal Communication Feedback:** Speakers often make mistakes or completely ignore interpreting an audience's verbal or nonverbal feedback.
- **Allowing the Audience to Take Control of the Speech or Speaker's Intended Message.** A speaker who allows an audience to take control of the content of a digital presentation creates avenues of audience disruption and can have difficulty getting back on topic. Speakers should develop a way to handle audience hecklers or disruptions in the speech.
- **Distracted Audiences:** The environment, location, personal media devices, and video conferencing platforms can distract audiences. If it is possible, attempt to reduce the potential distractions before the speech takes place.
- **Audience Knowledge on the Topic of the Digital Presentation**. If an audience already has preliminary knowledge of your topic, you should incorporate their knowledge and develop a more comprehensive speech topic.

Strategies to Improve Speaker Dialogue with Diverse Audiences in Digital Presentations.

- Always attempt to put yourself in the role of the listening audience.
- Understand that cultural communication competency is essential to the successful speaker/audience dialogue.
- Accurate nonverbal communication can many times be much more powerful than verbal communication.
- Adaptation of a speaker's style is important for audience comprehension.

- If you are provided the appropriate time or opportunity, research who will be present in the audience.
- Speakers who appropriately decode the audience's reaction during the speech can improve audience-message reception and improve understanding.
- Certain audiences can have a transformative aspect on the speaker and the speech. It is important that the speaker maintains the intended speech message and not allow the audience to change the message negatively.

In summary, as you may have noticed, a perfectly outlined digital presentation, which has been well researched and practiced, can only be successful if the speaker seriously considers who will be in the audience. Audiences during digital presentations and the feedback they provide are crucial to the speaker's success on presentation day. There are many aspects of audience analysis: individual demographics, attitudes, beliefs, and values. The presenter must inform, influence, and entertain audiences through well-crafted verbal and nonverbal communication. The presenter must consider the distance that a video platform can create with audiences and be able to adapt and respond to audiences needs. Successful digital presentations are very much an important skill set needed for all future employment, and may help you attain a place of employment or receive the promotion that you seek. Let us always realize the enormous responsibility the speaker has to observe, listen, and adapt to an audience in the most respectful and collaborative way to improve our digital presentations.

Tips for Conducting a Survey Monkey

How to gather information on specific audience wants, needs, and knowledge.

First, when approaching public opinion polling, a speaker should be aware of two types of research questions, quantitative and qualitative. Quantitative surveys and their questions provide hard data, percentages, or numbers. They show a speaker a clear consensus of the audience's wants, needs, and knowledge and can be valuable on basic demographic questions of race, gender, age, and so forth. The survey forces participants in the survey to choose from a prescribed list of answers.

ANALYZING THE AUDIENCE

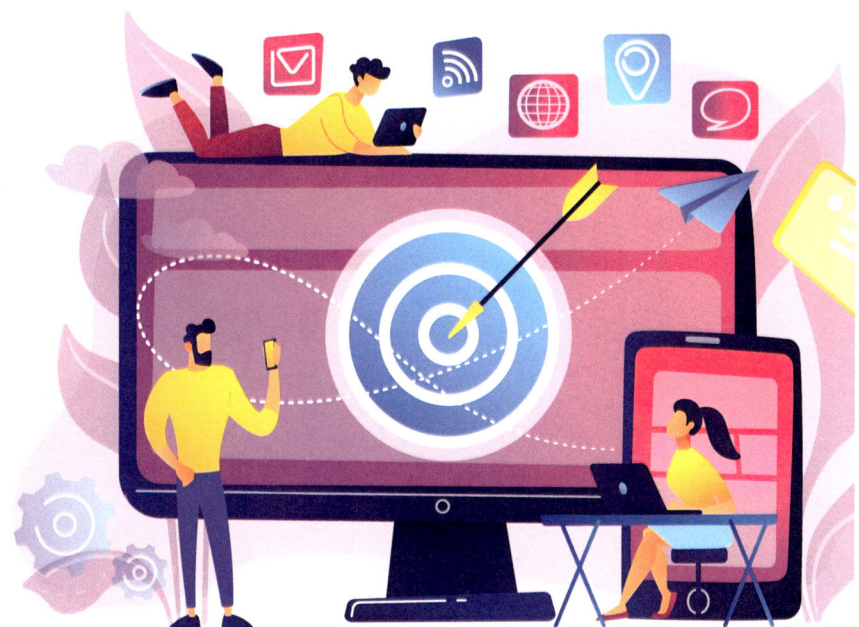

A qualitative approach allows for audiences to create many diverse types of feedback and is more individual in their response. It can be more time consuming or expensive to interpret this type of data. However, a combination of both can help a digital presentation gain insights into the wants and needs or previous knowledge an audience has on a specific topic.

How to Create a Survey
- Create a free account or log into your account. **http://www.SurveyMonkey.com**
- Once logged in, you should see a "Create Survey" button either in the middle of your screen or in the upper right corner.
- "Create Survey" takes you to a page where it will ask you some questions
  - Start from scratch- Import Questions
  - Start from template- Build it for me
  - Copy past survey
- It's easier and more customizable to build yourself
- Click "Start from scratch."

- Give your survey a name
- Choose a category
  - Choose a survey format
  - One question at a time
  - Classic
  - All questions on one page
  - Conversation
- Recommend either One question at a time or Classic
- Conversation can be complicated to write
- Choose one and click "Create Survey"
- Don't fall for the upsells!
  - Like logos
- **Page Title and Description**
  - The first thing people will see when they click on the survey
    - Make sure to thank them for completing the survey!
    - Tell them a little bit about what you're doing and why0
- **Save**
  - After filling in the title and description, click "save," and you're ready to create questions

How to Create Questions:

- Multiple Choice
    - Only one answer
    - Forces a choice from respondent
    - Can give ranges of answers
        - Which age category do you fit into?
            - 18-25
            - 26-40
            - 41-55
            - 56+
- Checkbox questions
    - Like multiple-choice, but allow for more than one answer
    - Should NOT have too many options
    - 5 or 6 maximum
    - More than that is confusing
- Matrix/Rating Scale questions
    - Ranges of frequency
    - Very poor to very good
    - Satisfied to dissatisfied

    "Use weights"

- Ranking
    - Want to know exactly how someone feels
    - Can find out favorites, but also seconds and thirds
- Single Text Box
    - Great for open-ended questions
    - Qualitative questions
    - Hard to interpret
    - Have to read all answers

How to review the final survey:

- At the top of Survey Monkey, you will see
  - Summary ➜ Design Survey ➜ Preview & Score ➜ Collect Responses ➜ Analyze Results ➜ Present Results
- Click Preview & Score
- See your survey the way your respondents will
- Go back to "Design Survey" and make any necessary changes

Sharing Survey with the Audience

- Click on "Collect Responses"
- Click on "Send Surveys Our Way"
  - Share a survey link
  - Post on social media
    - Lots of upgrades, but not necessary
- To control the posts and emails, click on "Share a survey link."
- Click on "copy" and share your link with others however you want.

How to Analyze Survey Results:

- After responses have been given, log back into Survey Monkey
- Click on the survey name
- Click on "Analyze Results"

These Survey Monkey results and the analysis of the results will go a long way for a digital presenter to gain a much better idea of what the audience already knows about your topic. Tailoring your presentation to the audience's unique attributes will establish speaker credibility, improve audience comprehension and keep the audience engaged throughout your presentation.

References

Dictionary.com. (n.d.). *Audience definition & meaning*. Dictionary.com. Retrieved August 3, 2022, from https://www.dictionary.com/browse/audience

Finding Information Online

Dr. Tracey Quigley Holden
University of Delaware

Public speakers, especially politicians, are often accused of offering their audiences nothing but hot air—lots of words and energy, but little content. To be an effective speaker, you must have more than enough information about your chosen topic to share with your audience. The way to find that information is to do research. Research might sound difficult or intimidating, but it is something you do every day. You gather information about topics you're interested in so you can make better choices. If you were considering taking a job, buying a car, or getting a roommate, you would spend time gathering and assessing information about your options. That is research! Research for a presentation should be more thorough and more selective than deciding on a restaurant to eat at this weekend, but both tasks involve the strategic acquisition of information.

In many train stations, metro stations, and even airports around the world, you will see signs and hear announcements telling you to "Mind the Gap." The gap in a train station is the space between the train and the platform, something you need to be aware of so you can cross it safely to get where you're going. One way to think about the information you need for your speech is to recognize existing "information gaps" you need to cross to reach your audience effectively. As you begin researching your topic, there is an information gap between what you know and what you need to know for your speech. There is also an information gap between you and your audience when you begin to present your speech. The gap between what you know, think, and believe about your topic and what your audience knows, thinks, and believes is what you want to bridge with the information you choose to include in your presentation. Recognizing these information gaps helps you think through the research process and begin to identify the information you need. You need to "Mind the Gap"! If you want to bridge an information gap, you will need to:

Gather the information you need about your topic;

Assess the information you find to determine its accuracy, quality, and appropriateness for your presentation;

Place the information in your presentation strategically so your audience has the best opportunity to understand your ideas.

Gathering Information

If you have ever felt like there was just too much information to take in, let alone to sort through, you are not alone. As far back as the 1660s, people noticed and complained about how much information was available. The term "information society" has become a common way of describing our current culture, and the burden of "information overload" is one we all carry. The concept of the information society emerged early in the 20th century, as the expansion of human knowledge moved toward an exponential pace. In the 1970s, the term "information society" was first applied as the economic impact of human knowledge and its distribution began to overtake the production of goods. (Crawford, 1983). In the years since the term was coined, the rate of information production and dissemination has only increased.

Research is done using **primary** and **secondary** sources. Primary sources are the original documents from history, accounts, or materials produced by people with first-hand experience.

Secondary sources are interpretations or analyses produced by people who did not have the experience themselves. Most of your research will be with secondary sources. Of course, you can do your **original** research as well. Speakers can sometimes **survey** their audiences to gain relevant information before a speech, such as an audience's knowledge about and attitudes toward a given subject. **The speaker could conduct interviews** to obtain first-hand accounts and comments from people with relevant experience or expertise with a topic area. However, in most cases, speakers must rely on secondary source research rather than original or primary source research as they look for information on their chosen topic.

The enormous increase in the amount of information available and all of the different sources of information noted above may seem daunting. But in the past fifty years, more and more information has been made available online. Project Gutenberg started digitizing books and cultural material in 1971 to offer free, global access to books (Project Gutenberg History and Philosophy, 2021). Material from books, journals, magazines, and other sources printed decades ago has been digitized and made accessible online, and nearly all new information is produced for online access. Although some publications are still behind paywalls, more and more researchers are posting their work publicly, and some research databases are opening their catalogs. Sites like z-library, libgen.li, and sci-hub allow users to download files of many books and journals, but they carry the risk of copyright or even ISP violations. Even so, a colossal amount of information is available at your fingertips, for free, if you have access to a computer and the internet.

Having so much information makes an effective strategy for gathering information one of the most important aspects of research. Thinking ahead and doing a little planning will significantly reduce the time you spend gathering information and improving the quality of the information you get. The saying, "Five minutes of planning is worth fifteen minutes of just looking," is even more true today than when E. L. Konigsburg wrote it in 1967 (Konigsburg, 1967). There are three steps to effective, strategic information gathering, and each one is described below.

1. Choose your search terms carefully.

2. Use the best available search tools.

3. Use your results to refine your search further.

Choose your search terms carefully. Our society now uses "Google" as a verb; most likely, you have "Googled" something recently. Google now processes over 40,000 search queries every second on average, translating to over 3.5 billion searches per day and 1.2 trillion searches per year worldwide, with each search producing hundreds of thousands of results. To make any search work for you, it should be focused and tailored to produce high-quality results. Starting with good search terms—the words and parameters you search for—is a critical step to finding good information. Knowing the topic you want to search for is a good starting point, but knowing a couple of related terms or possible subtopics is even better. Too broad a topic or search term will return too many results. Take five minutes to write down your topic's keyword or central phrase, and then add another three-to-five terms that are either directly related to your topic or indicate another area you are considering. For example, if your topic is "student activities," you might add "sports," "recreation," and "Greek life." Or you could start with "student activities" and add "funding," "diversity," and "campus culture." Using a combination of keywords and phrases will help you focus on your topic and will generate a stronger set of results from any search.

Usually, a search, especially in a public access search engine, such as Google, will produce more results than you can use. But if you don't get enough results, or if the initial results don't seem related to your topic, you need another approach. Changing your terms can produce very different results. It is important to keep in mind that the same topic can have several different names, and a simple change of terms could connect you to better resources. In the example above, "student activities" was the prime keyword. Another closely related term would be "student organizations" or "college clubs," which is when the concept of related terms can help you. If your initial keyword doesn't produce results, look for a synonym or a related term. Boolean *operators* are your friends. Boolean operators are the short words that connect your search terms into a searchable string. AND, OR, and NOT, with AND NOT used occasionally. Here is how they work when you have two related terms:

AND - tells the search engine to look for BOTH terms (Dogs AND Cats)

OR - tells the search engine to look for EITHER term (Dogs OR Cats)

NOT – tells the search engine to look for the first term but exclude items containing both the first and second term. (Dogs NOT Cats)

A search done using "prison reading programs," and one done using "prison AND reading programs" produce very different results within the same search engine. Substitute "correctional institution" for "prison" produces another set of results; trying "literacy" OR "reading" still another. As you work through your terms and combinations, you will likely see the same articles show up in multiple searches. Look at those articles first to see if you are getting the results you need.

Use the best available search tools. In the discussion of search terms, Google was an example of an effective and readily available search tool, which can get you **good** enough information. But in many cases, Google or other public access search engines will not produce the best possible results. Other information sites, such as about.com, ehow.com, and ask.com, have limitations that can lower the quality of the information you get. Online dictionaries and encyclopedias may offer a broad overview of a topic or a quick definition of a term for your personal use. Generally, they should not be used for more in-depth information.

For the most part, Wikipedia falls into this category as well. Wikipedia can be useful as a starting point to gain additional insights into your topic, to identify possible alternative search terms. It occasionally might have useful links to another more reliable source. These search mechanisms can provide you with a lot of information and sources to check. Still, they will also turn up a lot of junk and information from unknown, unverifiable, or poor-quality sources.

A **better** option is to use a search engine, which curates and reviews the indexed information. Google offers "Google Scholar" as public access but a limited-content search engine, which focuses on scholarly articles in recognized journals across a wide range of topic areas and scholarly disciplines.

Elsevier, Oxford University Press, Science Direct, and Wiley are all publishers of open access journals. Depending on your topic, searching in a scholarly and open access database could be very helpful. The articles and journals in these databases are usually peer-reviewed, which means experts in the field have read and approved the content, which can offer you a much higher caliber of information, especially for technical topics. Along the same lines, most industries have professional associations and publications within their field that offer well-edited, relevant information. These organizations and publications are geared toward people already working in that area who need to stay aware of important trends and innovations. If you are working on a related topic or have a strong interest in a particular industry, you should find out where professionals in the field look for their news.

If you have access to a good library, especially a college or university library, you may be able to use a database to do your search, which is almost always your **best** option for high- quality information. Some databases such as Nexus-Uni or General OneFile are wide-ranging, covering a huge variety of topics across tens of thousands of sources in popular media or publicly accessible records. Other databases, such as ProQuest and Academic OneFile, cover a wide range of topics and areas of knowledge but prioritize scholarly journals in their indexing.

Many databases are more specialized, covering a limited number of scholarly sources in a particular discipline. JSTOR, for example, indexes the contents of scholarly journals in the social sciences; including history, sociology, and political science. There are databases that only index newspapers, databases that index business and company information, and databases for science and medical information. *The New York Times* has digitized access to almost all of its issues going back to 1851, including advertisements.

Databases such as these offer access to high-quality information, often within a particular area of knowledge, and can include the most cutting-edge and recent research. Working in these databases can require patience and persistence. Unlike Google, where you can type in anything you want and start searching, scholarly databases often require you to set careful search parameters before starting to look. There can be layers of menu options to select from and multiple search terms to enter. Often you can set a specific date range, request only full text or peer-reviewed articles, even search for court cases or government proceedings. The process takes some getting used to, and what works in one database will not always work in another, but the overall quality of information is well worth the time.

Use your results to refine your search further. Once you have begun searching, you can do several things to help narrow and focus your results and sift out the best quality information. As you look at a results list, remember that most people never get beyond page 2. See how your results are reported. Many search engines and databases default to a ranking by "relevance," but how that affects your results can vary. It can mean only that the items at the top of the results had the most occurrences of your search terms. Viewing your results with different sorting criteria, perhaps in chronological order from newest to oldest, can help you identify the most current information.

Keep track of items that you have found that you want to review in more depth. If you are searching using a public search engine, it helps to open a file for notes and a folder for saving documents on your computer as you are searching. If you can open a file, keep a running list of the titles, authors, and, if possible, links to the most promising items. If you identify a document or an article that you want to review more carefully, download it and save it where you can find it later.

Most databases have a way to tag or mark items for later review; take advantage of that option if it is available. In some cases, you can have items emailed directly to you. With whatever approach you take, make sure your notes about your sources are complete enough that you can locate the item again. As search parameters change and as the search engines 'learn' what you're looking for, you can lose earlier items. Losing track of a good article is frustrating, and too often, it is impossible to recreate the search.
As you identify and review items, you can dig into them for additional pieces. There are links and lists of references to earlier research or related articles in scholarly articles and some Wikipedia entries. Especially in scholarly articles, those reference lists can lead you to the most important, earliest, or most reputable research in the area. They can also lead you to controversial issues and differences within a field. Either way, you have gained information and insight into your topic.

These strategies can and should be repeated until you have a reasonably large number of items to review. It is up to you to decide what is *enough* material to work with before you search again or move on to the next step. Putting time and effort into the information-gathering part of preparation is essential. As the saying goes, Garbage In, Garbage Out! Without good information to choose from, your presentation will not reflect positively on you as a speaker, nor will it help you bridge the gap to your audience. It's also helpful to review a few articles at a time rather than trying to plow through a giant stack. Knowing what you have and what you still need can help you search more effectively.

Assesing Information

When you have gathered several articles or sources, you are ready to review. Take a minute to consider your goals for your presentation. What do you want your audience to know, believe, or do after you speak? Having a clear sense of your goals as a speaker will help you look for the specific information you will use in your presentation.

The articles and other items you have gathered are raw information. What you want to pull out of that material is evidence. *Evidence* is the information you use to support the major claims and ideas in your presentation. Good evidence can stand up to close inspection, and all evidence should meet basic criteria before any of it is included in your presentation. You can use multiple types of evidence, and each type adds something a little different to your presentation.

Evidence also requires attribution; you have to let your audience know where you got it and who wrote or created it. Failing to provide correct and appropriate citations for your evidence is *plagiarism,* a form of theft with serious consequences. These three practices will help you identify the best information to include in your presentation.

- Evaluate the evidence carefully using multiple criteria.
- Choose a variety of types of evidence from your available information.
- Make sure you know the source of your evidence and cite it correctly.

Evaluate your evidence carefully, using multiple criteria. This evaluation step is the most important one you take in managing the information you have. You can't include all of the information available on your topic, nor would your audience want to listen for that long! Every presentation involves a selection process to decide what gets included and what gets left out.

Speakers have ethical responsibilities to their audiences to be accurate and honest. It is fine to present a particular perspective or to have an opinion about a given topic. However, ethically you must still ensure what you share with your audience is true, reasonably timely, and avoids obvious bias.

Evaluating your evidence for **accuracy** is the first criteria you need to apply, which can present some challenges, especially on controversial topics or with a topic about which not much is known. A good place to start is with the source itself. Where did your information come from? Is your source a reputable scholarly journal with peer-reviewed articles or a well-known source of current news? Within the article, can you determine how the information was created? Did the authors conduct their research, or are they reporting what someone else did? As you evaluate the information you have, it can help you look for facts or ideas in more than one source. That is not a guarantee, but it can indicate a higher likelihood that the information is accurate.

Assuming that the evidence you have is accurate, you will want to consider its **currency**. Generally, more recent information is most relevant to your audience and will add the most value to your presentation. With the fast pace of information creation and technological innovation, information from even two or three years ago is often obsolete or no longer applicable. If you are talking about a particular time in history or presenting a chronological perspective on your topic, then older information can still be relevant. But even if you were discussing the plays written by Shakespeare or the building of the Egyptian pyramids, it is a good idea to look for the most recent information available. New evidence and information still comes up on older topics and staying current matters more than ever before.

As you are assessing the **accuracy** and **currency** of your evidence, you should also consider the **relevance**. You could find a terrific piece of evidence, absolutely accurate and just out this week, but if it isn't relevant to your topic and what you want your audience to know, understand, or do, it isn't good for you. It is easy to get distracted by a compelling piece of evidence or an intriguing perspective you had not encountered before. Perhaps a great piece of evidence will make you rethink your approach to your topic or what you want to emphasize in your presentation! Be open to these possibilities. But as you are reviewing the information and looking for high-quality evidence, you should stay focused on your topic and presentation goals.

Depending on the time you have to speak, it is likely that you will be unable to include much of the evidence you find. Ask yourself, what will my audience get from hearing or seeing this? How does this support my ideas? Is it clear how this connects to my overall perspective on this topic? If you can answer these questions easily, you're on your way to a solidly supported speech.

Choose a variety of types of evidence from your available information. Once you have a collection of pieces of evidence, you will want to think about the types of evidence you want to include in your presentation. There are three major types of evidence, and each offers something useful and unique to your presentation. The three types are **statistics**, **examples**, and **testimony**. In your presentation, it is a good idea to include all three types to create a SET of excellent pieces of evidence within your speech.

Statistics are a powerful type of evidence using numbers to express information. Most statistics express a relationship, although often, the relationship is implied rather than explicit. According to the American Veterinary Medical Association, 36.5 percent of U.S. households own dogs and 30.4 percent own cats (AVMA, 2012). The statistic quantifies the relationship of pet-owning households to the total number of households. To put those percentages in more concrete terms, according to the AVMA, approximately one out of every three households in the United States owns at least one pet. Statistics are powerful because they tend to be accepted rather than questioned, and the use of numbers carries a tone of authority and competence.

Stephen Colbert coined the term "truthiness" to describe information that feels true, whether it is actually true or not. For many audience members, statistics feel true. As a speaker, you also gain credibility and authority when you use statistics effectively.

Statistics can make you sound more knowledgeable on your subject. For that reason, it is important to evaluate the statistics you use in your speeches carefully and to explain them clearly to your audience.

Statistics are generated from many sources for many reasons, and not all statistics are created equally. As with any piece of potential evidence, you want to make sure the statistics you use are accurate, current, and relevant. More specifically, make sure the statistic you use supports the claim you are making with it. For example, suppose your speech is about pet ownership. In that case, the statistic about dogs and cats could be useful to help your audience get a sense of how prevalent pet ownership is in the United States. Still, it does not say if those pet owners are responsible and care for their pets properly, nor does it account for households with multiple pets. It is up to you to determine if the statistical evidence supports your claim and explain the numbers to your audience in a way that makes sense but does not overstate or misrepresent the statistical evidence. Election polls are a good example of statistics that are often misrepresented or not fully explained. A poll will offer statistics such as Candidate A has support from 47 percent of the voters and Candidate B has support from 51 percent, and so Candidate B is the leader. But in small print, the same poll will indicate a "margin of error" of plus or minus 4 points. If the gap between the candidates is just four points, and the margin of error is four points, then the poll results are meaningless. Such examples of statistics with serious limitations and shortcomings are all too common. Again, it is up to you to find statistics that support your claims and explain what those numbers mean to your audience. The credibility and power of statistics can work to your advantage if you handle them well!

Examples are another form of evidence and probably the most commonly used form. Examples come in three forms: the **specific instance**, the **brief example**, and the **extended** or **narrative** example. The power of examples is in the way they help your audience to imagine and connect to your topic. Examples can create vivid images and evoke strong emotions for your audience members. They can act as the human-interest stories in the news, providing a connection to the personal experiences of your audience.

Specific instances are items on a list, usually given in sets of three. In your pet ownership speech, you might say, "The most common pets in the United States are dogs, cats, and birds." Those are specific instances. A list gives your audience the chance to identify with some aspect of your speech. While they might not own a dog, they might own a cat or a bird, and the list brings them into the speech and encourages them to continue to listen.

Brief examples are short stories, approximately three to five sentences long. Brief examples connect to our human affinity for stories. Stories build understanding, and a brief example can act as a small window into a new idea or concept. The audience can identify with the story in your brief example, even if the example is of something they have never experienced. The key to effective brief examples is to keep them short, vivid, and related to your topic. For example, for the speech on pet ownership, a brief example could describe a pet wedding. "Rocco and Brie spent $5,000 on food, fancy clothes, and themed decorations for their wedding last month. More than fifty of their close friends and family members gathered at Rocco and Brie's house to celebrate. When the groom walked around the room and sniffed all the guests, no one was worried — because Rocco and Brie are dogs." Such a short example paints a vivid verbal picture for your audience, helps them connect to your topic, and yet does not take up a lot of time. Brief examples are points of connection and understanding between you and your audience members.

The last type of example is the **extended** or **narrative** example. Just as it sounds, extended or narrative examples are longer and more detailed stories. The benefit of an extended example is the amount of detail you can include within the longer story framework. If a topic is particularly complex or difficult to understand, an extended example can be very helpful for your audience. However, extended examples also take much more time to deliver properly. If the example does not go over well with your audience, it can become a long and painful experience. It is also easy to get caught up in the details of a narrative example and miss the point of the story, especially if the example is a personal experience. No matter what type of example you choose, it should be vivid, help your audience connect to your topic, and clearly relate to the ideas and claims you want to make.

Testimony is another form of evidence that offers a unique contribution to your presentation. Testimony is evidence from someone with specific expertise or first-hand experience and is usually presented as a direct quotation. Carefully chosen testimony can be a powerful form of evidence, as it has both **authenticity** and **authority**. A good piece of testimony conveys the authority of the person you are quoting and the authenticity of someone's actual words. Testimony is commonly categorized into two major types – **expert** testimony and **peer** or **lay** testimony. Expert testimony most often comes from a person with recognized professional credentials in their area. The Surgeon-General of the United States or the Director of the Center for Disease Control would both have advanced medical degrees, perhaps additional credentials in public policy, and extensive experience with the policies and practices related to national health issues. They would be considered experts in public health.

Prestige testimony is a special type of expert testimony, often from an organization or person well-respected by other experts. The Mayo Clinic is a well-respected health organization, and statements from Mayo carry high credibility. Peer or lay testimony comes from a person with significant experience in a particular area, but not necessarily professional credentials or degrees. Basketball player Stephen Curry would likely be considered an expert on his sport, but he does not have a degree in basketball. His authority comes from his personal experience, and he could offer highly authentic peer testimony. Two key aspects for assessing testimony are the person's qualifications on your topic and the quality of their words. First, it is important to clearly and briefly explain the qualifications of the person to your audience.

You get credit from your audience for the quality of the testimony you use. You are borrowing the credibility of the person you are quoting. Additionally, you have the option to use a direct quotation or to paraphrase the person's words. If you quote the person, be sure that you are absolutely accurate in the quotation. Use the exact words, and make every effort to keep the quotation in the correct context. It is just as acceptable to paraphrase the person. Unless the quotation is so good or so striking that you cannot even come close to matching it, often you can convey the same information in your own words.

The famous quotation from John F. Kennedy's 1960 inaugural address, "My fellow Americans, ask not what your country can do for you; ask what you can do for your country," is so iconic and so powerful, there is no good way to restate it. Kennedy also spoke about the importance of physical fitness and was a strong proponent of the President's Council on Physical Fitness. During his presidency, Kennedy expanded and promoted the program. His support was a significant factor in the program's success and recognition of the importance of fitness, especially for school children. In a 1961 speech supporting the program, Kennedy said, "Physical fitness is not only one of the most important keys to a healthy body, but it is also the basis of dynamic and creative intellectual activity." This is a strong quote, but it could be reasonably and effectively paraphrased to "Kennedy viewed physical fitness as an important part of creative and intellectual work as well." Use quotations when they are so great or so eloquent, you can't possibly say it any better; use paraphrases when the quotation is good, not great, and can be effectively restated.

Make sure you know the source of your evidence and can cite it correctly. While doing your research, keep track of the sources of the information. You will need to know the author, the publication name or site, and the date your source was published. If you are using information from a website, you need the URL and the date and time you accessed the site. Given the likelihood of a link being taken down or revised, that combination allows reasonably precise identification of your source.

Oral citations are often different than the written references given at the end of a paper or in the closing visual aid of a formal presentation. You should ALWAYS give attribution for any information that you did not create yourself, including images in your visual aids. Bear in mind that the abundance of material available on the internet or through social media does not mean you can use whatever you find. Many images, website materials, and other accessible forms of information are protected by copyright. Even if no copyright is present or asserted, never use anything you find without crediting the source. YouTube videos, Vines, tweets, Instagram photos, blogs and Facebook posts are examples of public sources that still require citations for anything you use.

In digital presentations, it can be difficult for the audience to see the citations on your visual aids. If that's the case, you may choose to provide a reference slide at the end of your presentation and orally cite the sources for your visual content in your speech. For oral citations, you want to provide your audience with enough information to find the source if they wanted to get more information. Sometimes this will mean giving the entire formal reference orally; more often, you can give the most relevant and necessary information about the source without formal reference. This abbreviated form of citation allows you to speak more naturally and stay in the flow of your presentation. For example, if you are citing an article written by Nicholas Kristof in the *New York Times,* you might not include the author in your oral citation, but instead say, "In a *New York Times* article from May 21, 2016...." If your topic is relevant and your audience is familiar with Kristof's work as a journalist and advocate, you might want to cite him more directly, "In May 2016, Nicholas Kristof's column in the *New York Times* covered....." Both oral citations will let your audience know that the material came from a credible source and where they could find more information; neither is a complete and formal reference. As noted above, failing to cite your sources properly is plagiarism.

Placing Information

When you have gathered and assessed a substantial collection of possible pieces of evidence, it's time to work through the process of deciding what to use and how to place it in your presentation. You already know that the different types of evidence offer different benefits within a presentation. It's also important to consider your audience's abilities to understand and process information. We know that the average rate of speed for a speaker is about 100-175 words per minute, and we know that the average listener can take in about 300 words per minute. But those rates do not factor in the time it takes to understand and evaluate information that is unfamiliar, of high interest, or verbally complex. So here is another gap for you to bridge—the gap between your speech rate and your audience's ability to understand.

One good way to think about how much evidence to include is a concept known as the Magical Number 7, Plus or Minus 2 (Miller, 1956). Miller's concept suggests that most humans can manage about seven pieces of information at one time. Here, "manage" means to understand, hold in short-term memory, and put in context. In more (or less) challenging situations, or with audiences who are more (or less) capable or interested, the number rises to about nine or drops to about five. As a speaker, you can be thoughtful about how much information you give your audience at any one time and how you can place it within your speech to maximize comprehensibility, which is accomplished in three ways: by limiting how much evidence you include; by "chunking" your information to maximize audience comprehension; and by positioning your strongest evidence for maximum effect.

First, select the best possible evidence, limiting the total amount of evidence you present. Knowing that each type of evidence offers different benefits, you will want to try and choose what to include based on the quality of the content and the effect of a given type of evidence. Too much of any one type of evidence can seem unbalanced and sound awkward. For most speeches, choosing various types of evidence to create a **SET** is an effective approach. Creating a **SET** for your speech means you have included at least one or two pieces of each type of evidence: **S**tatistics, **E**xamples, and **T**estimony in your speech. A more technical speech would likely have more statistics, a speech to share an experience, more examples or testimony, but creating a **SET** gets you off to a good start.

Second, "chunk" your information into fewer pieces and give your audience clear cues about the "chunks" you have created for them. Using an outline can be very helpful in this process. As you think through your main points, subpoints, and the supporting evidence you want to include, you are already chunking your information. The structure of a typical speech or essay—introduction, three main points, conclusion—effectively chunks information into just five pieces. Within each of the major sections, information can be added in a similar pattern. For example, one of your main points could include two subpoints, each with two pieces of supporting evidence.

Even adding an opening and closing statement within that main point still gives you only eight pieces of information to convey to your audience. With good signposts and verbal cues from you, your audience will process those eight pieces and associate them with your main point, which turns the eight pieces into one chunk, freeing up processing capability. Now your audience is ready and able to take in more of your great information!

Finally, think about the overall goal of your speech and what evidence you have that most powerfully supports that goal. Listeners tend to recall the first and last things they hear, a result known as the "primacy–recency effect." Additionally, listeners tend to recall more details about recently heard information (Crano, 1977). Depending on your topic and content, placing the strongest basic concepts at the beginning of your speech and more specific details at the end might be an effective strategy. It also helps to repeat and restate the important concepts you want your audience to remember long after you've concluded your presentation.

Conclusion

In this chapter, we discussed the basic principles and strategies for effective research and information gathering. Understanding the "information gaps" that must be bridged for your presentation to be effective is a basic building block of effective communication. Three key concepts have been presented to help you "Mind the GAP."

Gather the information you need about your topic;

Assess the information you find to determine its accuracy, quality, and appropriateness for your presentation;

Place the information in your presentation strategically so your audience has the best opportunity to understand your ideas.

With these concepts and the accompanying strategies, you have the tools you need to do effective research for your presentations. In our information society, the ability to gather, assess, and place high-quality information is a critical skill. This chapter has provided the directions you need to navigate through your information gathering effectively and efficiently.

References

Dictionary.com. (n.d.). *Audience definition & meaning*. Dictionary.com. Retrieved August 3, 2022, from https://www.dictionary.com/browse/audience

Crano, William A. (1977). "Primacy versus Recency in Retention of Information and Opinion Change." The Journal of Social Psychology. 101(1) pp.87-96. DOI: 10.1080/00224545.1977.9923987

Crawford, Susan. (1983) "The Origin and Development of a Concept: The Information Society." *Bulletin of the Medical Library Association,* 71 (4) pp. 380-385.

The history and philosophy of project gutenberg, by Michael Hart. Project Gutenberg. (n.d.). Retrieved August 3, 2022, from https://www.gutenberg.org/about/background/history_and_philosophy.html

Konigsburg, E.L. (1967) From the Mixed-Up Files of Mrs. Basil E. Frankweiler. New York, NY: Dell.

Miller, George A. (1956) "The Magical Number Seven, Plus or Minus Two: Some Limits on Our Capacity for Processing Information." *The Psychological Review,* 63, pp. 81-97.

U.S. pet ownership statistics. American Veterinary Medical Association. (2012). Retrieved August 3, 2022, from https://www.avma.org/resources-tools/reports-statistics/us-pet-ownership-statistics

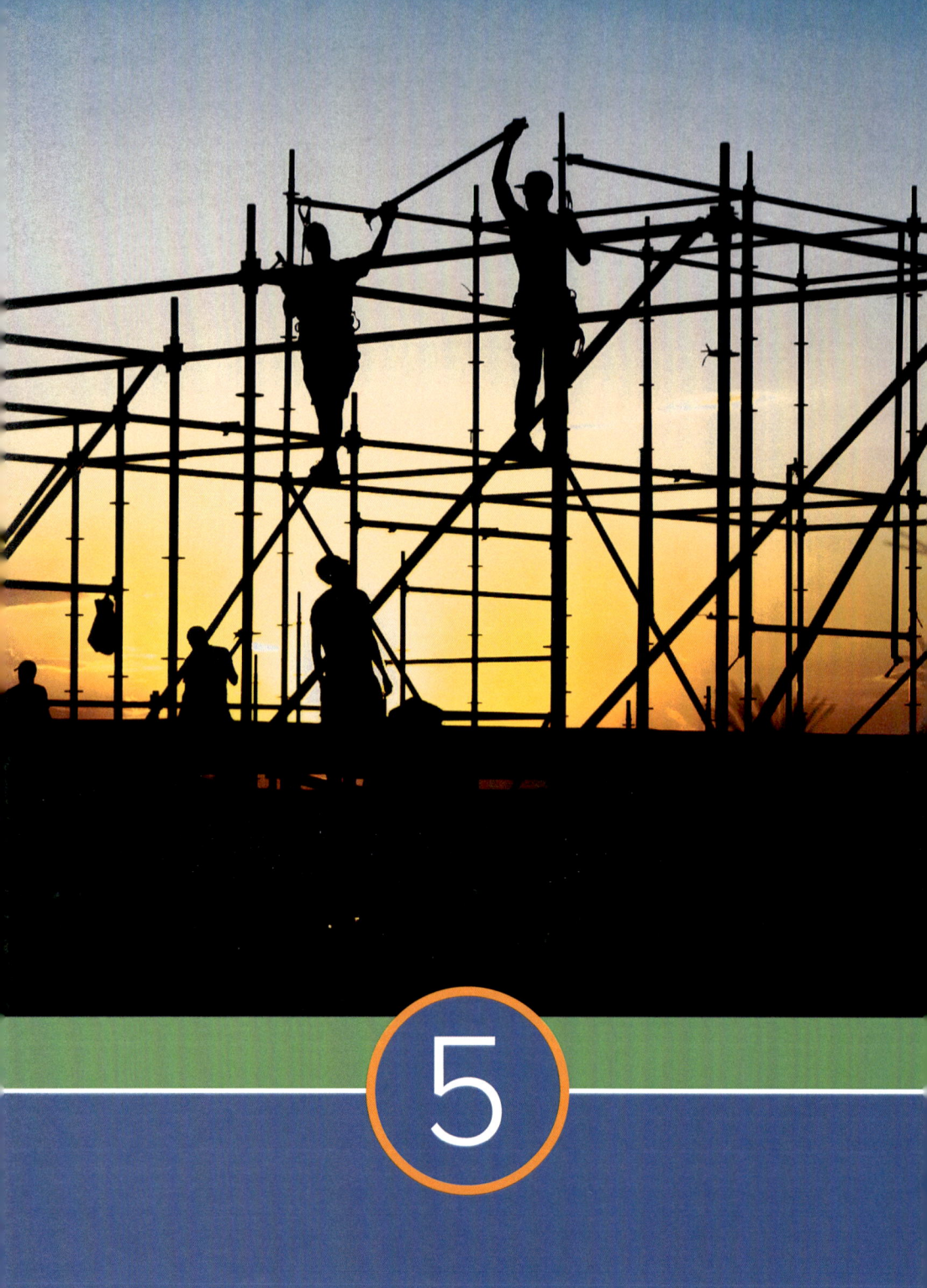

Planning and Organizing

Sandy French
Radford University

Effective digital presentations require thoughtful and methodical planning and preparation. In the online environment, presentations can often seem rushed and lack the careful planning that comes with traditional face-to-face presentations. This chapter covers key aspects of planning and outlining digital presentations, and touches on issues of security and accessibility.

Planning and Outlining

Effective presentations in any format begin with solid research, audience analysis, and planning. A presentation cannot be well organized if you are unsure what you are talking about! After thoroughly researching a topic, presenters must be clear on what they want to share with their audience. Have you ever listened to a presentation and thought, "I don't get it?" Sometimes presenters have so many ideas they want to share with an audience that the listeners are unclear about what to take away from the presentation. How does a presenter gain clarity about what it is they really want to communicate to an audience? Try answering this simple question: "When I'm done with my presentation, I want my audience to know that _____."

The second portion of the sentence is the main message of your presentation, and the presentation should be organized so that all the research and information you provide help the audience remember this main point. Creating one sentence that captures the essence of a presenter's purposes is trickier than it sounds. Too often, presenters fail to realize that this simple step is the key to organizing a message. Given all the knowledge you have acquired on your topic through your research, how will you zero in on the essence of what is most important? As Cary Nieuwfof says, "It takes far more work to be clear than it does to be confusing" (Nieuwfof, 2015). For example, let's say you are doing a presentation about baseball. Here's an example of identifying the main idea of a presentation:

INEFFECTIVE MAIN IDEA: To inform my audience about baseball.

EFFECTIVE MAIN IDEA: When I'm done with my presentation, I want the audience to know that baseball uses three main skills.

Once the main idea is established, it's time to figure out how many main points are needed to communicate the main idea effectively. Ideally, presentations of any length contain no less than two and no more than five main points. Make sure that each piece of support you provide fits well into your main points. If not, you are wandering away from your main idea! When crafting your main points and the evidence you will use to support them, keep in mind the principles of **discreteness**, **parallelism** and **progression**.

Discreteness ensures that your main points are distinct and do not overlap. When deciding what supporting materials to use, if an idea or piece of evidence can fit into more than one main point, the points are not discrete enough. Each main point should contain unique information that supports the overall goal of the presentation.

Parallelism means keeping the same or similar importance or scope on all the points made. Using parallelism will help keep your main points balanced so that each main point takes up roughly the same amount of time. For example, perhaps you are giving an informative presentation about automobile care. Using similar phrasing for your main points keeps them "parallel." Too often, students might use phrases such as "To check the oil," which is not a parallel construction.

i. Checking the oil
II. Changing a tire
III. Cleaning the inside

By keeping each main point to a three-word phrase that starts with a "C," you are helping your listeners clearly understand your main points.

Progression is the logical ordering of the main points. Effective organization of supporting materials provides a logical and smooth flow to your presentation. Presentations that are well organized are easier for the presenter to deliver and for the audience to understand. Again, a presenter needs to ask one main question, **"What's the best way for me to show the relationships among my materials?"**

As you prepare your presentation, using proper **superordination** and **subordination** will help you to see any issues you might experience with discreteness, parallelism, or progression. When outlining, the *Superordinate* is the top main point. In a traditional outline, the top main point would be next to a Roman numeral. *Subordinate* ideas are subcomponents of the main point. In a traditional outline, these would be next to capital letters.

How to Make an Outline

Once you have developed your main idea and started conducting your research, outlining will help provide you with a roadmap to give your audience a clear picture of the beginning, middle, and end of your presentation. Just like map directions on your phone provide you turn-by-turn instructions, a clear outline guides the audience step-by-step through your information. By organizing presentation content in a structured form, you can more easily show your audience a hierarchy of ideas and relationships among them without crafting a "word for word" memorized presentation. Outlines allow you to present in a methodical, but more relaxed format providing more opportunities to connect with the audience.

When outlining your presentation, ask the following questions:

1. What am I talking about?
2. What am I trying to accomplish?
3. Which 2 – 5 main points will best help me accomplish my goal?
4. What is the logical order of these main points?

As you answer these questions, present your information in outline form. The symbolization and indentation should look like this:

I. Main Point (Supraordinate)

   A. Subpoint

   B. Subpoint

      1. Sub-subpoint

      2. Sub-subpoint

II. Main Point (Supraordi

   A. Subpoint

      1. Sub-subpoint

      2. Sub-subpoint

   B. Subpoint

      1. Sub-subpoint

      2. Sub-subpoint

Using an outline structure will help you create a presentation that is clear, concise, and balanced. To summarize, when outlining:

- Start with main points
- Break into sub-points
- Create Introduction
- Create Conclusion
- 5-10 words for each main point and sub-point is enough to speak spontaneously
- You don't want a "script"
- You need to connect to your audience

Once the body of the presentation is finished, you will need to work on your introduction and conclusion.

Introduction

The beginning of a presentation is often the hardest to create. Have you ever heard the saying that it only takes seven seconds to create a first impression? (Goman, 2011). Your introduction is your first impression. Use it to pique the interest of your listeners and establish common ground. Too often, presenters give little time and attention to how they will begin a presentation, opting instead for the strategy of simply stating, "Hi, I'm Sandy, and today I'm going to talk to you about ways to reduce pollution." This type of introduction generates little enthusiasm from listeners and fails to convey a presenter's genuine interest in sharing information with listeners. Effective introductions help create a favorable first impression with listeners and generate interest in your presentation. By starting off well, effective introductions can also boost your confidence as the presenter. What is an audience looking for in an introduction? Effective introductions include the following elements:

1. Grab the attention of the audience
2. State your topic/purpose
3. Relate topic to the audience
4. Preview the body of the presentation

Step One: Grab the attention of your audience. While presenters have several options for introducing a presentation, we will focus here on five key ways to make an impact:

1. Ask a question
2. Share a startling fact or statistic
3. Use a relevant quotation
4. Tell a humorous story or joke
5. Use a real or hypothetical example

Ask a question. When a presenter begins with a question to the audience, the answer is usually obvious, but asking the question makes a point. If you are presenting an informative presentation on cancer, you might ask audience members to stand up if they know someone affected by cancer. This type of visual "answer" could help a presenter show the widespread impact of the disease and set the stage for the presentation. However, a presenter must analyze the audience adequately to have confidence in the answer listeners will supply to the question. For example, during one public speaking class that I taught, a student wanted to convince his classmates to ride the university-provided bus transportation around campus rather than drive their cars to protect the environment. He researched the percentage of students who drove to campus daily rather than using the bus system, and he felt well prepared to give his presentation. However, he neglected to analyze the particular audience to whom he would be speaking—his classmates. As he began his presentation with the following question, "How many of you drive to campus to get to your classes?" he anticipated a large number of students to nod in agreement or perhaps even raise their hands. Unfortunately, he was met with puzzled looks because this particular class was composed of freshmen who were not allowed to have cars on campus and who already used the bus system! It was a painful eight minutes of listening to him trying to convince the audience to do what they were already doing—riding the bus around campus.

Using a question to attain your listeners' attention need not involve them standing, raising hands, or answering out loud. Another method is to use **rhetorical questions.** Rhetorical questions are those questions asked where you do not expect a response. Still, they create a certain effect within the audience, including displaying or emphasizing the presenter's opinion on a topic. Rhetorical questions can effectively attain an audience's attention if you have confidence that your listeners will answer (silently or otherwise) in the way you expect. Perhaps you might ask: Do you ever have a problem when two major papers are due on the same date?

Share a startling fact or statistic. Providing a startling fact or statistic can attain the audience's attention by jolting the audience out of complacency. For example, one student began her presentation on clean drinking water this way:

> I see several of you brought water or something else to drink to class today. How long did it take you to get that drink? Probably not very long. We basically can get clean water whenever we want it, but in many areas of the world, this is not the case. In countries that lack access to clean water, women and girls spend up to six hours daily collecting water. That's more time than a student taking a normal load spends in class daily! .

Sharing a startling fact or statistic as a method of attaining an audience's attention is most effective when not overplayed. Don't overdramatize the situation; present the facts in a clear and compelling manner. Often, when we start with a startling fact or statistic, we need to pause and let what we have said "sink in" for our audience. The idea is to cause your listeners to reflect.

Use a relevant quotation. Starting a presentation with a relevant quotation can provide a theme or frame to the rest of your presentation. Often presenters will use a quotation from someone famous, but the most important point is that the quotation be relevant to your presentation. Starting with John F. Kennedy's famous "Ask not what your country can do for you, but what you can do for your country" might make sense in a presentation about volunteering, but be less relevant to a presentation on spring break vacations. Where can we find useful quotations? Of course, you can search the internet for famous quotations, but did you know some books compile this information for you? Check out *Barlett's Famous Quotations* or *The Oxford Dictionary of Quotations* in the reference section of your library. The index at the end of the book provides a way to find topical references by muliple authors.

Tell a humorous story or joke. When telling a joke, keep in mind "the grandma rule." If you wouldn't tell the story or joke to your grandmother, you probably shouldn't tell it to the audience!

Similar to quotations, keep the story short, simple, and relevant. Also, keep in mind that an attention-getter should use your strengths as a presenter. If you routinely forget the punch line when telling jokes to your friends, this may not be the opener for you! Like quotations, you can find jokes in books, magazines, and online, but they should be relevant to your presentation. For example, when my daughter ran for a position in student government at her school, her presentation emphasized her skills as a problem-solver. She decided to open her presentation with a relevant joke: "What did one math book say to the other? We've got problems!" Be sure your joke is clean, easy to deliver, and relevant to the topic.

Use a real or hypothetical illustration. An illustration could be a real story, a story from literature, or even a plausible tale. As other options for attaining an audience's attention, the story must be relevant to the main point of your presentation. Such stories can come from newspapers, magazines, sermons, and your own life experiences. For example, one student used just such a story when giving her informative presentation:

> I'm leaving a late-night movie with my father when suddenly, as he's driving, we hear it and see it. Those dreaded lights and sirens! My father pulls over, and the police officer politely asks him if he's been drinking. With slurred speech and the smell of alcohol on his breath, my father responds, "No, officer." At that moment, if my father had been arrested for drunk driving, he could have died. You see, my father wasn't drunk but slipping into diabetic shock. Nearly 29 million people in America are diabetics. Today, I will share with you some information about diabetes: its causes, symptoms, and treatments.

This student used a personal illustration to great effect. She grabbed her audience's attention by drawing them in with a true, personal, and cleverly told story.

Step Two: State your topic/purpose. Presenters should clearly explain the topic they will be presenting. Leave no doubt in listeners' minds exactly what you will be speaking about: "Today, I will share with you the benefits of learning a foreign language in college." Focus on providing the topic statement in one clear, concise sentence, "Today I will be sharing with you how to spot the warning signs of a stroke." Your specific purpose guides the content and organization of the main points of the speech. There should be no confusion as to what you will be presenting about. Step two provides a road map of your topic and how it will be organized.

Step Three: Relate to the Audience (WIIFM). "WIIFM" stands for "What's In It For Me?" Effective presenters must let their audience know what they can gain from listening to your presentation. After establishing your authority to speak on a subject, you can further enhance your credibility by explaining to the audience how listening to your presentation will benefit them; how the information you share will be relevant to their lives. Consider the presenter who states, "While I have enough money to buy a yacht or two, I think many of you have to consider your spending habits more carefully." By getting the audience to laugh at the absurdity, the presenter wins them over to consider what she is about to relate.

Step Four: Preview the body of the presentation. The final step is to preview the main points you will cover in the body of the presentation. For example, once you know the presentation is about the benefits of learning a foreign language, it is important to know how the presenter plans to discuss those benefits and how many benefits will be discussed. The preview statement helps listeners stay on track and follow the presenter: "I want to share with you three benefits of learning a foreign language while in college: enhanced cognitive function, improved multitasking, and increased employability upon graduation."

Be sure to include all four steps for an effective introduction: gaining the attention of your audience, clearly stating your topic, relating your topic to the audience, and previewing the body of the presentation.

Conclusions

Like introductions, presenters often neglect the conclusions of their presentations. Students sometimes end presentations by thanking the audience for their time or asking for questions, but these are not effective endings. A solid conclusion reviews the presentation's main points and leaves the audience with a sense of closure. A transitional word or phrase, such as "finally" or "to conclude my presentation," usually precedes the ending of a presentation. Follow these steps to prepare an effective conclusion:

Return to your introduction. Consider the mood you wish to create in your audience in the final moments of your presentation. What techniques are available to help a presenter create a memorable ending? You may refer to your introduction in some way. Remind the audience of the interesting information you provided to begin your presentation, "bringing them around" full circle at the end. Consider what you want your audience to do or think after your presentation. State that in your conclusion.

Summarize your main points. Audience members, even engaged ones, can sometimes drift away or momentarily daydream. A brief summary of your main points reminds the audience of the key ideas of your presentation. Your introduction includes a preview of your main points – the conclusion provides a review of those same points. This repetition increases the likelihood that audience members will retain those points after the presentation.

Provide your audience a final takeaway. A final takeaway provides a sense of closure and finality. It can also inspire or challenge an audience. Here are some examples of how one might provide closure and a sense of finality in conclusion.

- Provide an appropriate quotation
- Challenge your audience to do something
- Return to a story or joke from your introduction

Provide an appropriate quotation. Similar to gaining the audience's attention in your introduction, you can use a quotation to bring a note of finality to your presentation. For example, a presentation about the benefits of active listening might end with the proverb: "We have two ears and one mouth because listening is twice as important as talking." A brief and relevant quotation at the end of a presentation can stir an audience and help them reflect on the information you have just shared.

Challenge your audience. Particularly when doing a persuasive presentation, a challenge to the audience to do something can make for an effective and emotional conclusion. For example, suppose a presenter is trying to persuade the audience to get involved in the worldwide lack of clean drinking water. In that case, a challenge to the audience to donate the money they typically spend on bottled water in a week could be an effective call to action.

Return to a story or joke from the introduction. Returning to a story or joke you mentioned in your introduction provides coherence to your presentation. One student gave a presentation on the problem of human trafficking and started her presentation this way:

> 43,200. That's the number Karla Jacinto told the CNN reporter to remember. It's the number of times Karla was raped during her time in captivity due to human trafficking. That's thirty men per day, seven days a week, for almost four years.

After giving a stirring and disturbing informative presentation on the current state of human trafficking, the student returned to Karla's story for the conclusion:

> Karla is now twenty-three years old. She's told her story to the U.S. Congress, the Pope at the Vatican, and speaks out at conferences and events aimed at stopping human trafficking. But Karla is one of the lucky ones. She escaped. Won't you get involved to help others like Karla?

These three strategies for ending a presentation with the appropriate mood you wish to create can be used separately or together.

Your conclusion creates the final impression in the minds of your audience. Don't leave it to chance. Carefully plan out your conclusion and practice it, so you are ready to leave a forceful and lasting impression on your audience.

Organizational Patterns

There are many organizational patterns available to presenters. The same topic, organized differently, will produce a drastically dissimilar presentation. Which one you use will be guided by the type of presentation you are giving.

Here is an illustration of this point using a popular topic: Walt Disney. We will see how a presentation about Walt Disney looks quite different and provides diverse information based on the organizational pattern chosen. If your purpose is to **inform** or **teach**, consider using a *Chronological, Spatial* or *Categorial* pattern.

Chronological. A chronologically organized presentation is arranged according to time. This organizational pattern works well for presentations that take an audience through the history of a person, place, or idea. For example, a presentation about the life of Walt Disney lends itself to a chronological organizational pattern, with main points easily divided into periods.

MAIN IDEA: When I'm done with my presentation, I want my audience to know that Walt Disney spent much of his life failing before he succeeded.

BODY:

I. Disney's early years were impacted by war. (1901-1918)

II. Disney's early cartoons were a string of failures. (1919-1928)

III. Disney's successes were unpredictable. (1929-1966)

This chronological organizational pattern divides Walt Disney's life into decades and takes the listener through his failures and successes from birth to death. Other organizational patterns might include some of the same research but have a different focus.

Spatial. A spatial organizational pattern follows a direction. A spatially organized presentation, in effect, makes you the tour guide for your audience. A presentation about Walt Disney that focuses on The Walt Disney World, for example, could be spatially arranged as you take your audience through each separate park or on a tour of one particular park, say the Magic Kingdom. Presenting a presentation using a spatial pattern would include different and additional information from a presentation using another organizational pattern.

MAIN IDEA: When I'm done with my presentation, I want my audience to know that there are five main sections of the Magic Kingdom.

BODY:
I. Main Street, USA

II. Tomorrow Land

III. Fantasy Land

IV. Liberty Square

V. Frontier Land

The spatial organizational structure works well for describing some types of landscapes, such as a theme park, the D-day beaches of the Normandy Invasion, or an archaeological site.

Categorial. The most commonly used organizational method is a categorial or topical organizational structure, where you divide a larger subject into logical subtopics. There is no right or wrong way to divide a topic; just use ways that make sense given your overall main purpose for the presentation, and try to employ **The Rule of Three**. Organizing in triads or trios often makes things easier for an audience to remember.

MAIN IDEA: When I'm done, I want my audience to know that marriage rituals are different in China than in the United States.

BODY:
I. Chinese wedding attire

II. Chinese wedding banquet

III. Post-wedding rituals

Notice the logical structure of the body of the presentation and that each main point is an independent idea. The topical organizational structure can be used for almost any subject and is the most frequently used of all organizational patterns.

If your purpose is to **persuade** or **motivate**, consider using *Monroe's Motivated Sequence* or the *Effect-Cause-Action* patterns.

Monroe's Motivated Sequence. Monroe's Motivated Sequence is a five-step organizational pattern of persuasion. This organizational pattern is meant to inspire the audience to make changes. When using this pattern, a presenter emotionally motivates an audience to take action. Many infomercials follow this organizational pattern. The five steps are: attention, need, satisfaction, visualization & call to action.

Attention: This is your introduction. Start by grabbing the attention of the audience with a startling statistic or fact relevant to your overall topic. When picking your attention getter, consider what you know about your audience – who they are, what they may know about your topic, and what they might find most interesting or unusual.

Need: This is where you explain the problem. Clearly explain to your audience what the problem is and why it is a problem. The audience should see themselves in the issue establishing the problem or need as their own.

Satisfaction: Once you establish a need/problem for your audience, you must show them how to satisfy their need. What are the steps the audience should take to resolve the problem?

Visualization: Now that the audience knows a problem exists, see that the problem applies to them, and has a clear understanding of the steps necessary to resolve the problem, the visualization step explains to the audience how much better their lives will be if they implement your solution. Focus on the benefits – to the immediate audience, as well as to the larger society – of how much better their lives could be if they implement your recommended solution.

Action: This is the final step of the organizational pattern and is your conclusion. Here you urge your audience to take immediate action to resolve the issue. A call to action should be simple, clear, and manageable for your audience. Examples of a call to action include: signing a petition, no longer buying a particular product (like single-use plastic), or attending a rally. Monroe's Motivated Sequence is a tried and true method for motivating and persuading audiences. However, it is not the only option available.

Effect-Cause-Action. The Effect-Cause-Action pattern of organization is particularly useful when giving persuasive presentations because it shows the relationship between various conditions and their impact, as well as telling the audience how they can help. When using the Effect-Cause-Action structure, a presenter might choose to discuss various causes (reasons) first, then explain their effects (consequences). However, a presenter can also discuss the effects first and explain the causes second. Either way, the pattern ends with an action step that explains how the audience can help alleviate the problem. Suppose you were giving a presentation about the lack of worldwide access to childhood vaccines. Your presentation might start with why vaccinations are not readily available worldwide, then discuss the effects of non-vaccination, and conclude with ways to contribute (either time or money) to organizations making a difference in worldwide vaccination.

Conclusion

In this chapter we have discussed how to plan, organize, and outline your presentation. Whether you are informing or persuading, no matter what pattern you use, remember to target your audience. Consider what you know about your audience, and tap into your audience's values and emotions. By carefully following these guidelines for digital presentations you can avoid many of the pitfalls presenters face.

References

Goman, Carol K.(25 Feb. 2022). *"Seven Seconds to Make a First Impression."* www.forbes.com. Retrieved August, 2022, from https://www.forbes.com/sites/carolkinseygoman/2011/02/13/seven-seconds-to-make-a-first-impression/?sh=56e851f42722

Nieuwhof, C. (2022, February 28). *7 ways communicators kill their messages (and how to avoid the traps).* CareyNieuwhof.com. Retrieved August 2022, from https://careynieuwhof.com/communicators-kill-messages/ .

Connecting With Your Audience Emotionally

Patricia A. Coughlan
Rowan University

Using Emotion

Think about a time when you experienced communication that used emotion as a means to an end. Were you watching a late-night program? Did an ad pop up showing neglected, starving animals caged or facing unrelenting rain, snow, or heat? Did sad music play in the background while a well-known actor's voice asked you to imagine the animal's plight and to donate just a few dollars to improve that animal's life?

Or, where you watching the Super Bowl when an ad featured an adorable puppy who befriends a horse? Not just any horse, the recognizable, symbolic, Anheuser Busch brewing company's Clydesdale horse. And, then the ad sentimentally develops a story of friendship where that horse protects that puppy from wolves and assists that puppy in finding its way home?

Commercials and popup ads, and not just those sponsored by the American Society for the Prevention of Cruelty to Animals or Budweiser's popular heartwarming Super Bowl spots, understand the power of emotion to connect with an audience. Emotion persuades.

Long before ads and commercials, some millenniums ago, the ancient Greek philosopher Aristotle pondered the use of emotion to persuade audiences. In, **The Art of Rhetoric**, Aristotle identified three modes of persuasion:

Ethos – the speaker's character and credibility

Pathos – the speaker's use of emotion

Logos – the speaker's use of logic or reason

Aristotle saw all three modes as essential tools for influencing an audience's acceptance of a message. Pathos, though the second mode, has no less importance than Ethos and Logos. Each mode has the power to persuade. In fact, many messages that lack evidence, reasoning, and logic, still succeed because the passionate, emotive filled words of the speaker persuade the audience to act.

Think of the English words that derive their meaning from the ancient Greek root pathos. Humans have the ability to express sym**pathy**, em**pathy,** or to show no emotional connection - a**pathy**. As Aristotle explained, Pathos is the ability to move individuals by establishing an emotional connection, a common bond. Your goal is to invoke your audience's emotion as a means to an end, not to create apathy.

Understand the Emotions of Your Audience

By now you have heard about the need to be **audience centered**. As defined audience centered refers to the effort you expend analyzing an audience to increase your ability in crafting a message that guides an audience to a specific outcome. By researching your audience's demographics (age, gender, religion, sexual orientation, group affiliations and racial & cultural background), and considering their attitudes, beliefs, and values you will be able to reflect upon the audience's receptivity to your message and adapt it appropriately.

Humans are wired to feel. Our senses continually gather information that help us make decisions. Over the course of an average day, humans respond emotionally to countless situations. The ease at which this response happens makes us view emotion as a relatively simplistic experience. Yet, it is not. Before an emotion is recognized consciously by us or is apparent in our response to others, our body has completed a series of complex physiological and chemical processes that result in a behavioral response. Each time we feel or show emotion, our bodies' organs, neurotransmitters, and limbic system have been engaged.

Now you might not recognize the physiological changes occurring in your body as you manifest an emotion but you are wired for it and have been since the dawn of humanity. The limbic system is the most primordial portion of your brain. Often called the "lizard brain", since the limbic system is the limited brain function lizards possess, the phrase refers to the basic ancient human practice of fight or flight. Left over from our early human origins, the limbic system functions in response to perceived stimuli which in turn activates our basic emotions; for early humans this was an adrenaline rush and the decision to stay and fight or to flee the danger in order to survive, to live, and to cave paint about it another day.

This Photo by Unknown Author is licensed under CC BY

A physiological adrenaline response, often characterized by a racing heart and sweaty palms, the limbic system boosts your energy in response to an emotional need. Now in every situation you encounter, you are not fighting or fleeing to survive, but your body is still responding emotionally through the same primordial limbic system. How we interpret those emotions is now determined by our thinking mind. The physiological response may be the same, but now we recognize the feeling, assess it, apply context, name it, and manage it. Our ability to name it is an act of communication.

Consider these two scenarios....

Scenario 1 – Each night when you finish working at the library, you walk home by the exact same route. However, on this night there is a new cement sidewalk that is still wet in your way. You could walk in the street, but as it is dark, and the street is not well-lit, you decide to take a different route. While walking this new route you hear footsteps behind you. What do you do?

Scenario 2 – Each semester many of your classes required you to give a short group presentation. You even work the guest desk at your gym. You love to talk to people in small groups or one on one. It seems natural. However, you do not like to speak to larger groups because when you were in middle school, a classmate laughed when your visual aid fell over during a presentation. The class laughed too. Fall course registration is now due and there is a public speaking class required for you to graduate. You know the course requires you to give four longer speeches in front of an audience. You could sign up for the course now, as you are only a junior, or you could put it off until another semester. What do you do?

Can you see how in each scenario you are facing a fight or flight decision? If you respond only through your emotions, you could over or under-react. However, if you engage your thinking mind and analyze your emotional response, you can create a more reasoned response.

Pathos = Emotion

In, *The Art of Rhetoric,* Aristotle identifies emotion as states of mind that invoke pleasure and pain and thus influence human perception and behavior. Human emotions fall into four categories:

- Fear
- Anger
- Sympathy
- Aspiration

Understanding these emotions can be utilized by a speaker to effectively connect the message to the audience and to call the audience to action. However, it is important to point out that your understanding of human emotion should always be applied ethically. The National Communication Association's (NCA) *Credo for Ethical Communication* reminds us that as ethical communicators, we need to be truthful, accurate, honest, and reasoned to maintain communication's integrity. We must endorse "freedom of expression, diversity of perspective, and tolerance for dissent to achieve the informed and responsible decision making fundamental to a civil society" (NCA Legislative Council,1999, reaffirmed by the NCA Legislative Assembly, 2017). Though separated by millenniums, Aristotle espoused the same ethical concerns as the NCA. In his discussion of pathos, Aristotle cautions against the misuse of emotion to distort an audience's understanding or opinion. To make his point, Aristotle metaphorically compares the misuse of emotion to the action of a person measuring distance using a crooked ruler. The analogy equates "knowingly using the crooked ruler" to "deliberately measuring distance with that crooked ruler"
as an unethical act that creates distortion and inaccuracy. That would be manipulation. Manipulation is the act of intentionally, unfairly, and even unscrupulously playing upon someone's emotions for your own gain. Ethically using pathos is not manipulation. Be accurate and ethical in your use of pathos.

crooked ruler : mismeasuring distance :: unethically using pathos : manipulation

How Can You Evoke Emotion in Your Audience

In his TEDTalk, *The Clues to a Great Story* (2012), Pixar film director, screenwriter, producer and actor, Andrew Stanton stresses the notion of using audience message. He says, "Make them care." Essentially Stanton is saying that your goal in appealing to emotion is to connect with your audience. This connectivity will make them more receptive to your message. Now take time to watch Andrew Stanton's talk: After listening to Stanton, you care. He makes evoking emotions in others seem so easy. He got you to care. But Stanton is a well-established Pixar storyteller. How exactly do you make your audience care?

It begins with audience analysis. Effective audience analysis will result in a greater understanding of the people with whom you are communicating. Using that understanding to frame your message will result in you honoring your audience's views while increasing the likelihood your audience will understand your message and feel the same thing that you, as the speaker, feel about the topic. Effective pathos establishes a bond with your audience. This bond will help the audience:

- understand your message.
- accept your message.
- act upon your message.

Using the Four Basic Emotions

Fear — a feeling that someone or something is a threat or dangerous.

How to Use with an Audience

- Ask them to Imagine a future (not too distant).
- That imagined future needs to include something the audience does not want to happen.
- This will stimulate the limbic system and invoke fear in the audience.
- Why would you want your audience to be fearful? Because now you will give them a solution/something they can do to take away the fear.

Anger – a strong feeling of annoyance, displeasure, or hostility.

How to Use with an Audience

- Establish a scenario that is based on a violation of an audience's expectation.
- This scenario is more effective if it threatens a right or privilege.
- This will invoke anger in the audience.
- Anger seeks justice. There are two types of justice: **Retaliatory** and **Compensatory**.

  Retaliatory Justice – refers to justice that seeks to "even the score", to punish, to cause suffering, is retaliatory, and revengeful. You **do not want** your audience to seek retaliatory justice.

  Compensatory Justice – refers to justice that seeks to provide equitable recompense and fair compensation for an unjust wrong. **You do want** your audience to seek compensatory justice.

  Why would you want your audience to be angry? Because it will drive them to take an action seeking compensatory justice, one that you may suggest, that could fix the situation and turn the anger into positive productivity. Many social justice movements that have created lasting social change started because of anger.

Sympathy – a feeling of sorrow or pity for someone else's circumstances, usually a misfortune.

How to Use with an Audience

- Establish a scenario that asks the audience to picture and perceive another person's pain and/or misfortune.
- This scenario is most effective if the pain is unjust or undeserved.
- This will invoke sympathy in the audience by pulling on their heartstrings.
- Why would you want your audience to be sorrowful? Because it will drive them to take an action, one that you may suggest, that could reduce the sorrow for other individuals. Many humanitarian and aide organizations depend on sympathy to seek financial aid and volunteers to support their missions.

Aspiration – a feeling of hope to achieve some desired outcome, a call to do better.

How to Use with an Audience

- Establish a scenario that asks the audience to visualize how they can take an action to improve ourselves, our lives, or our world.
- This scenario is most effective if the scenario makes the audience feel as if they deserve the outcome of the action.

- This will invoke aspiration or hope in the audience.
- Why would you want your audience to be hopeful? Because it will drive them to visualize a better world where their action, one that you may suggest, could improve life. Many advertisements depend on establishing aspirations in viewers which then motivates viewers to buy the product which they think will improve their daily lives.
- Monroe's Motivated Sequence is a great strategy for invoking aspiration.

What is Monroe's Motivated Sequence

In the mid-1930s Purdue University psychology professor, Alan H. Monroe used his understanding of psychology and human behavior to study how humans respond to persuasive messages. In his book, *Monroe's Principles of Speech,* Monroe presents an organizational strategy consisting of five key steps that persuades and motivates an audience through emotion. Professor Monroe's strategy is often viewed as a variation of problem/solution. The five steps of Monroe's Motivated Sequence are:

1. Attention – the speaker engages the audience through a well-designed attention getter (evoking emotion).
2. Need – the speaker establishes a "need" (a problem) that appeals to the audience's psychology (a chance to use sensory detail to make emotional connections).
3. Satisfaction – the speaker offers a viable fix for the need (a solution to the problem).
4. Visualization – the speaker now offers detailed scenarios asking the audience to picture themselves as being part of the solution (creating emotional buy in).
5. Action – the speaker calls the audience to take action and be part of the solution to achieve satisfaction.

The effectiveness of Monroe's Motivated Sequence lies in its ability emotionally to connect with the audience. The speaker who uses Monroe's approach makes the audience feel as if their experiences and emotions are valued and that the speaker cares about how the audience feels on the topic being presented.

Using Language to Evoke Emotion

Noted American author and humorist, Mark Twain once wrote, "The difference between the almost right word and the right word is really a larger matter; it's the difference between the lightening bug and the lightening." Twain reminds us that well-chosen words give a speaker power over an audience.

Time and time again, strong, image evoking, sensory words that engage, make meaning, and create memory, have cast spells over audiences. A few powerful words like, "I have a dream that my four little children will one day live in a nation where they will not be judged by the color of their skin, but by the content of their character" (Martin Luther King Jr, 1963), live on well after they are spoken.

After her near death at the hands of extremists, the human rights activist, Malala Yousafzai, penned in her memoir, *I Am Malala: The Story of the Girl who Stood Up for Education and was Shot by the Taliban* (Little Brown & Co., 2013) a message to all speakers. She wrote, "When the whole world is silent, even one voice becomes powerful."

Use your voice whether in written or spoken words to evoke emotion. Your well-chosen words can powerfully touch hearts, change minds, and transform the world.

Two highly effective language strategies to evoke emotion in your audience are **Imagery** and **Narrative.**

- **Imagery —** When you hear the word imagery you often think of poetry's figurative language use and the sensory detailed written word, but imagery is for the spoken word too. What you say can create sensory pictures in the mind of your audience. Paint mental pictures with your words. Use your words to create visually descriptive, vibrant, detailed, sensory images that will engage your audience.

Consider this poem...

The Red Wheelbarrow
by William Carlos Williams

so much depends
upon

a red wheel
barrow

glazed with rain
water

beside the white
chickens.

Can you see how the words of this poem create visual, sensory images?

When using imagery avoid clichés, overused phrases that lack original thought. You have heard, *"You can't judge a book by its cover", "the grass is greener on the other side"*, or *"a big fish in a small pond."* Though these phrases sound creative, overuse makes them trite and insignificant. Be inventive with your words and invoke emotion in your audience.

- **Narrative** – When you hear the word narrative you should immediately think of a narrator, someone who tells a story. Effectively using storytelling as a means to engage your audience through feeling is essential. Good storytellers make you care about the character(s) by providing important and significant details that evoke emotions and create memories. Since the dawn of humanity, people have been programmed to enjoy stories. The individual who can tell a story that connects to an overarching message has a powerful tool to engage and motivate an audience to action. A powerful narrative can be used many ways within your presentation. You can use it as your attention getter, a way to illustrate an idea or point within the body of your presentation, or as an effective way to close. Wherever you choose to use a story make sure it is used to emphasize and complement your overall message.

All stories share some key elements that establish a recognizable pattern for your audience. Make sure to incorporate these narrative elements.

Narrative elements:

1. **Setting** – the location of the action, both place and time.
2. **Characters** – the individuals the story is about and with whom the audience will identify.
3. **Action** – (also called plot) the events and actions that comprise the story. The action has a noticeably clear beginning, middle, and end with an established conflict that the characters need to resolve.
4. **Manner** – the ways in which the characters approach the conflict and try to solve the problem, how does it happen.
5. **Outcome** – (also called the resolution) the results of the overall action.
6. **Theme** – the message the storyteller is trying to convey. What did the character(s) take away from the story? What was the lesson learned? What is the overarching idea? How does it connect to the audience?

Good narratives are directed towards one point and have strong structure. As you heard in Andrew Stanton's TED Talk, "knowing your punchline, from the first sentence to the last, is leading to a singular goal, and ideally confirming some truth that deepens our understandings..." (TED, 2012).

Narrative that allows an audience to identify with characters, builds tension, utilizes detail, and provides a satisfying outcome increases the opportunity to engage the audience. Through descriptions of locations, visualization of characters, detailed explanations of actions, and words that establish mood through emotions like excitement and suspense, a good narrative can connect the audience to the storyteller's overall theme. But remember, the narrative you tell is *not* your presentation. Instead, it is a vehicle by which to make a point about your message and to evoke emotions in your audience. Use narrative deliberately but do not overuse it!

A bonus strategy that can be effective if done well is **Analogy**.

- **Analogy –** An analogy is a comparison between two things. The attributes and characteristics of a complex item is applied to another item to simplify and clarify a relationship as a means to create audience understanding. In his TED Talk, *The Mystery of Chronic Pain (2011),* Dr. Elliot Krane uses the feelings associated with a feather and a blow torch to make an analogy between the mild pain and the chronic pain his patients feel.

feather : mild pain :: blow torch : chronic pain

Dr. Krane incorporates imagery, narrative, analogy, and the appropriate use of jargon with definition to emotionally connect with his audience and to broaden their understanding. Now take the time to watch Dr. Elliot Krane's TEDTalk as way to consider language use.

Remember as you incorporate emotional language into your presentations beware of **Jargon**. When you present to an audience, you are the expert. Since your grasp of the topic is more expert, it results in you knowing a lot of technical and content specific vocabulary related to the topic. You speak the jargon!

Jargon – is the highly specialized words or expressions that are associated with a specific field. Often jargon is considered the "professional language" that insiders in the field know. Outsiders of the field or individuals from other professions are unlikely to know the terminology.

When giving a presentation you cannot avoid jargon. As the expert, you need to use the technical terms of the topic, however your responsibility is to explain the jargon. A single word such as "phlebotomist" would be jargon from the world of medical hematology (the study of blood), so too would be a series of steps in a process like "viticulture", "vinification", "fermentation", and "maturation" which are all steps in the winemaking process. Whether the vocabulary is a term or a process, if it is technical jargon, you must explain it to your audience. The best way to do this is to say the term and then translate it into plain speak or general language. Here are some examples:

phlebotomist – While I was at the doctor's office, the *phlebotomist*, the person who takes your blood, put a bandage on my arm after my blood test.

viticulture – The first step in winemaking is *viticulture*, the process of growing grapes.

vinification – The making of wine, also known as *vinification*, was practiced by the Ancient Romans.

fermentation – The key process in winemaking is *fermentation* when sugars are converted into alcohol.

maturation – Newly fermented red wine is placed in oak barrels to go through a *maturation* or developing period before it is bottled and ready to drink.

In each of the sample sentences provided, the additional words and phrases help clarify the meaning of the jargon term. Knowing who is in your audience will help you decide which terms you need to define. Make every effort to increase your audience's understanding of your words. Failure to do so will aggravate, bore, or anger your audience and cause them to disengage.

Using Emotion to Make an Argument
What is an Argument?

Almost everything is an argument. A piece of text, spoken word, or visual that expresses an opinion (whether blatant or subtle) is an argument. Arguments present a stance and attempt to persuade. Many arguments are easy to spot. As readers, watchers, and listeners, we often sense when someone is using language to persuade us. An ad, like the one at the start of this chapter, about animal cruelty clearly is arguing for us to help support animals in need. Its level of argument and persuasion is obvious. Likewise, during election season, political ads and speeches are examples of blatant argument and persuasion. Yet some arguments are more subtle. While watching the opening monologues late-night television hosts Jimmy Kimel, Jimmy Fallon, or Stephen Colbert, we may believe we are being entertained. But is that totally true? Is that the single purpose of the monologue? Many of those monologues are full of opinions and views that make us laugh while also expressing an opinion that provokes and persuades us to think. When talking about argument we are not talking about two individuals in a heated debate, instead we are discussing rhetorical argument.

Argument – is a rhetorical process that attempts to persuade an audience by utilizing ethos (credibility), pathos (emotion), and logos (reasoning) to adopt a certain position or stance.

An argument is stated as a claim that is backed by reasoning and evidence. A claim is the conclusion you are asking your audience to draw from the information and evidence you present. The claim is overarching idea you want to convince your audience to accept or to act upon.

There are three types of claims, value, judgement, and policy.

Claims of Value: consider the moral, ethical, and aesthetic worth of an idea, concept, object, or process. Value claims ask the audience to decide if something is *good* or *bad*, *right* or *wrong*, *better* or *worse*.

Example: The capital punishment is morally and ethically wrong.

Example: Renaissance works of art by DaVinci and Michelangelo are better than Cubism works of art by Picasso and Dali.

Claims of Fact: consider the truth or falsity of an assertion. Fact claims ask the audience to decide if something is true or false.

Example: Climate change is the biggest threat to humankind.

Claims of Policy: consider whether rules, requirements, or laws, need to be enacted or changed. Policy claims ask the audience whether a course of action ought, should, or must be changed or taken.

Example: Universities and colleges should not be allowed to enforce policies that require all freshman and sophomore students to live in on-campus housing.

A good argument has a strong organizational pattern that shows how ideas connect with evidence and research while using reasoning to support the claim. Incorporating emotion can help engage the audience with the topic.

Every day information can be crafted as a message that expresses an opinion, makes an argument and establishes a claim.

Consider this scenario...
Hurricane forecasters are predicting the 2021 hurricane season to be above normal. In 2020 the Atlantic hurricane season was abnormal and made the record books. The season saw 30 named storms and 12 direct strikes, both new records. In fact, after using up all the letters A through Z in the English alphabet, hurricane forecasters had to use the Greek alphabet to name storms. Leaving broken infrastructure, economic plight, food shortages, sanitation issues, and personal loss in their aftermath, hurricanes are one of the most damaging of natural disasters. OXFAM International, whose mission is to fight inequality to end poverty and injustice, says the number of climate-related disasters, like hurricanes, have tripled in the last 30 years (oxfam.org).

Do you feel...
Fear – because it might mean that this is a not an anomaly and that climate change is escalating.

Anger – because world leaders and international organizations should be doing more to discover what is causing the increase in hurricanes and to help those in need after hurricanes hit.

Sympathy – because you can empathize with the people and communities impacted by hurricanes.

Aspiration – because you might want to be part of the solution and help solve the causes and minimize the effects of hurricanes.

Can you see how this scenario has the ability to evoke all of these feelings which could be used to engage an audience in argument?

Can you see how this scenario has the ability to be crafted into a claim of value, fact, or policy?

Arguments About Policy Change

Policies influence our day-to-day actions. Whether found at work, in our community, within our nation, or throughout the world, public policies affect the average individual. Arguments about policy change are important because they challenge rules and question how rules operate in the real world. A change in existing policy or the creation of a new policy can help or hinder our lives. Since humans either embrace or resist change, policy arguments spark debate. Someday you may need to call for a new policy or challenge an existing policy. Thus, it is important to understand how to craft an argument calling for policy change. The Stock Issues Model is an effective strategy to utilize when seeking policy change.

Stock Issues Model

The Stock Issues Model is a recognized process of formal debate that is used to analyze and identify the elements of an issue that cause a clash of ideas or argument. It is characterized as a commonsense approach for managing change. It recognizes that debate is a natural component of a democratic society. Any time the status quo is challenged, the person challenging the status quo needs to establish that there is a problem, explain the causes of the problem, and then propose the benefits of a solution (a new policy or change of policy) to solve the problem. Change causes disagreement and The Stock Issues Model proposes a standard way of addressing the common or "stock" ways that disagreement occurs. The Stock Issues Model has four components.

1. **Significance:** establishes the reasons for the debate. Considers the problem and the harms Items caused by the problem. This stage asks you to consider:
   - What's wrong?
   - What's wrong right now?
   - Why is there a sense of urgency?
   - Is this issue big enough or bad enough that it demands action?
   - Is there a "quantitative significance"?
   How much, how many
   - Is there a "qualitative significance"?
   The impact; a harm to people's lives or a harm to society

2. **Inherency:** explores the actual situation and the reason for the status quo. Considers the why status quo exists. This stage asks you to consider:
   * Why is this significant harm happening?
   - Structural inherency -
     Is there any kind of law, policy, or formal structure that makes the harm continue?
   - Attitudinal inherency -
     Is there an attitude, belief, value, or emotion that makes the harm continue?
   - Existential inherency –
     The harms exist and the status quo is not able to solve the harms. It is what it is.

3. **Plan:** proposes the actions needed to change the status quo. This stage asks you to consider:
   - Who should do what? (consider the stakeholders)
   - Who should have the power to make change (agency)?
   - What should be something they can accomplish?
   - How will the new change be enforced?
   - Is funding needed?

4. **Solvency:** presents the advantages of the planned changes. This stage asks you to consider:
   - What evidence can you use to show the audience that if they do what you want them to do, the harms will be significantly reduced?
   - How your plan solves the problem?
   - Can you show how the degree of solvency matches the degree of change you are requesting?
   - Are there any additional advantages to the planned changes?

The Stock Issues Model recognizes that it is natural for humans to debate issues. It establishes a plan for you to successfully advocate for policy change. For the model to be most effective, you need to conduct a full analysis of the status quo, conduct research to support your claims, and establish why change is necessary to reduce the harms associated with the status quo. The model lends itself to the use of ethos (credibility) to establish good will, logos (reasoning) to show evidence and support for the needed change, and pathos (emotion) as a tool to evoke emotion and transform your audience into fellow policy change advocates.

Chapter Conclusion

In this chapter we have discussed the importance of emotion to messaging. By considering how our earliest ancestors responded emotionally by fighting or fleeing, we gain a greater understanding of why humans emotionally respond first and reasonably respond second. Our ability to analyze the emotions of fear, anger, sympathy, and aspiration allows us to use Aristotle's concept of pathos to center our messages on our audience and engage them emotionally. Remember your choice of words, with attention to imagery, narrative, analogy, and jargon paired with strategies like Monroe's Motivated Sequence and the Stock Issue Model will evoke emotion in your audience, create effect arguments, and if used responsibly will impart engaging and ethical messages.

References

King, M.L. (28, Aug. 1963). I have a dream [Speech transcript]. American Rhetoric. https://www.americanrhetoric.com/speeches/mlkihaveadream.htm (original work 1963)

Krane, E. (n.d.). *The mystery of chronic pain.* Elliot Krane: The mystery of chronic pain | TED Talk. Retrieved August 17, 2022, from https://www.ted.com/talks/elliot_krane_the_mystery_of_chronic_pain?language=en

Monroe, A.H. (2017). Monroe's principles of speech. Forgotten Books. (original work published 1951)

National Communication Association. (2017). NCA Credo for Ethical Communication – National Communication Association. https://www.natcom.org/sites/default/files/Public_Statement_Credo_for_Ethical_Communication_2017.pdf.

No more delays: *Help us avert famine in East Africa.* Oxfam International. (n.d.). Retrieved August 17, 2022, from https://www.oxfam.org/en

Stanton, A. (n.d.). T*he clues to a great story.* Andrew Stanton: The clues to a great story | TED Talk. Retrieved August 17, 2022, from https://www.ted.com/talks/andrew_stanton_the_clues_to_a_great_story?language=en

Yousafzai, M., Sākonthat, S., Lamb, C., & Yousafzai, M. (2558). *I am malala.* Matichon.

7

Ethics in Online Communication

Sheena Howard
Rider University

Considering the Ethics of Online Communication

The National Communication Association is the most influential communication group in the United States, with more than 8,000 communication scholars and practitioners (Abbott, Timmerman, McDorman, & Lamberton, 2016). In 1999, the association published its credo that outlines ethical communication behaviors in communication in the public and private sphere. We will examine this credo relating to online communication, providing us with an overview of the implications and practices of ethics across the field of communication.

NCA Credo for Ethical Communication
(approved by the NCA Legislative Council, November 1999)

Questions of right and wrong arise whenever people communicate. Ethical communication is fundamental to responsible thinking, decision making, and the development of relationships and communities within and across contexts, cultures, channels, and media. Moreover, ethical communication enhances human worth and dignity by fostering truthfulness, fairness, responsibility, personal integrity, and respect for self and others. We believe that unethical communication threatens the quality of all communication and consequently the well-being of individuals and the society in which we live. Therefore we, the members of the National Communication Association, endorse and are committed to practicing the following principles of ethical communication:

- *We advocate truthfulness, accuracy, honesty, and reason as essential to the integrity of communication.*

- We endorse freedom of expression, diversity of perspective, and tolerance of dissent to achieve the informed and responsible decision-making fundamental to a civil society.
- We strive to understand and respect other communicators before evaluating and responding to their messages.
- We promote access to communication resources and opportunities as necessary to fulfill human potential and contribute to the well-being of families, communities, and society.
- We promote communication climates of caring and mutual understanding that respect the unique needs and characteristics of individual communicators.
- We condemn communication that degrades individuals and humanity through distortion, intimidation, coercion, and violence, and through the expression of intolerance and hatred.
- We are committed to the courageous expression of personal convictions in pursuit of fairness and justice.
- We advocate sharing information, opinions, and feelings when facing significant choices while also respecting privacy and confidentiality.
- We accept responsibility for the short- and long-term consequences for our own communication and expect the same of others.

Source: National Communication Association. Credo for Ethical Communication. 1999. https://www.natcom.org/uploadedFiles/About_NCA/Leadership_and_Governance/Public_Policy_Platform/PDF-PolicyPlatform-NCA_Credo_for_Ethical_Communication.pdf

Although this doctrine is from the late 1990s, before the advent of the current online tools we now have available, communication principles are just as, if not more, relevant in the current digital sphere. Online communication allows us to exercise the option of anonymity, both as a speaker and as a receiver of communication. You can choose to deliver or receive a message in the digital sphere without disclosing your identity. Therefore, online communication is a tool that can be used in a different and sometimes more unethical way than face-to-face communication.

Some might argue that the principles of the NCA credo are even more important in the digital space because we all have the potential to use our messages to reach a wider number of people and affect a larger number of people with our communication. We now have access to individuals all over the world. We need to take that ability seriously and maintain the utmost adherence to ethical standards. For example, the National Communication Association addresses the importance of truthfulness, unity, and the power of the word when addressing ethical considerations of communication. These considerations are also specific to online communication and important for students new to the field of public communication.

In the age of social media and digital communication, the likelihood of your presentations and conversations being recorded and posted on third-party electronic websites or apps is a reality. Therefore, ethically speaking and researching are of great significance.

As you can identify in the qualities described by the National Communication Associations' credo, the following are important as they relate specifically to ethics and online communication:

- Plagiarism
- Respecting the Message
- Being inclusive
- Respecting Your Audience
- Respecting Yourself

These topics are helpful in our understanding the nature of ethics and online communication and showing you how you can **practice** the ethics of communication in the digital sphere. This process or practice of ethics in online communication is made easier by our ethical standards. Ethical standards, or moral principles, are the set of rules we abide by that make us "good" people and help us choose right from wrong. Consider the following practices of ethics (Millner and Price, 2016).

Throughout this chapter, we will use the foundational criteria established here to provide concrete tactics for incorporating ethics into the process and delivery of messages in the online environment, which will not only make you a better communicator in the digital space but will also shield you from the possible embarrassment of the consequences related to unethical public communication practices. These consequences could include the following: removal from one's job, loss of friendships, being shamed and smeared via social media, failing a college course or being expelled from school, among other things.

The Practice of Ethics in the Digital World

As a public speaker, you should take seriously the responsibility you have as a public communicator and the consequences of your communication. Below are five core ethical public speaking ideas and behaviors that you should consider. These core principles will conclude this chapter and prepare you for the research, writing, and delivery phases of the digital public speaking process.

Plagiarism

Plagiarism is using someone else's work or ideas without giving the source credit or acknowledgment. When it comes to online communication, we often become inspired by the content others post or others' ideas that we want to incorporate into our messages, which should be encouraged; however, even in the online environment, you must always cite or give credit to the source whenever you use someone's idea or work.

More explicitly, a plagiarist is a person who is appropriating authorship illegally, and most importantly, deliberately, and that is theft. The word plagiarism most likely comes from the Latin word "plagium," which is translated as "theft." And the theft of someone else's property is nothing more than a crime and is strictly prosecuted by law (Copyleaks, 2020).

A study by Dr. Donald McCabe and The International Center for Academic Integrity (2021), conducted between 2002 and 2015, found that an overwhelming majority of undergraduate students, graduate students, and high school students have plagiarized or cheated on assignments and exams. Research shows that social media and the prevalence of online communication boost the likelihood of cheating or plagiarism. According to a 2020 article on Copyleaks.com, Google registered more than 75 million copyright takedown requests in 2016. These notifications were related to writing, music, images, and movies. Today, the internet is full of all kinds of information. We can find anything; enter the right words in the search box. On at least one occasion or another, most people reading this have copied and pasted social media posts or even sentences into assignments or documents without sourcing the content creator. It is exceedingly easy to copy and paste information, making the likelihood of plagiarism more prevalent. As a creator in the online environment and a student creating digital presentations, we need to be especially mindful of this ethical reality. Let's break down the reasons behind plagiarism in the online environment, as well as the three distinct types of plagiarism.

Types of Plagiarism

Global Plagiarism

There are three distinct types of plagiarism – global, patchwork, and incremental plagiarism (Lucas, 2011). **Global plagiarism**, the most obvious form of plagiarism, transpires when a speaker presents a speech that is not his or her own work (Millner and Price, 2016). Plagiarism is particularly easy to catch in the online environment when people can record your speech and upload the text to applications and websites that can easily detect plagiarism.

Patchwork Plagiarism

According to Millner and Price, 2016), **patchwork plagiarism** occurs when one "patches" together bits and pieces from one or more sources and represents the result as his or her own. Michael O'Neill (1980) also coined the term "paraplaging" to explain how an author uses the partial text of sources with partial original writing. Again, this is made easier by copying and pasting text and paragraphs from online articles into our own assignments. Incremental plagiarism

Incremental Plagiarism

The third type of plagiarism is **incremental plagiarism**, which occurs when most of the speech is the speaker's original work. Still, quotes or other information have been used without being cited. Incremental plagiarism can occur if, for example, you provide a statistic to support your claim but do not provide the source for that statistic (Millner and Price, 2016). Again, this is prevalent in the online environment, as people copy and paste quotes from others across social media platforms without always citing the source. However, just because there is no way to penalize each person engaging in plagiarism does not mean it is ethical, good or right to engage in this practice. These considerations lead us to discuss *why* social media increases the prevalence of plagiarism and how you can decrease the likelihood that you will be engaging in plagiarism in the online environment.

Intended Plagiarism

Marketing and promotion are exceedingly popular online. Brands both big and small want to "go viral;" therefore, they want you to share their content. For example, when self-published authors or companies issue a press release online, their goal is to get the media and individuals to reshare it to spread the news about what they are selling or marketing. In essence, brands want you to plagiarize so that their content or product(s) reaches as many people as possible., This practice creates an ethical dilemma as *intended plagiarism* essentially allows us to get used to or comfortable with reposting or resharing content without necessarily citing the source. However, as an effective and ethical communicator, you need to be especially mindful and intentional not to cite the source (or brand) from which your messaging comes.

Convenience and access

No prior period in human history has allowed us to access the volumes of information and data that we have today. This access to information is not showing any signs of slowing down. As discussed, social media and online communication have made it exceedingly easy to access large amounts of information, including published papers, others assignments, and day-to-day messages that might aid us in writing speeches or completing academic assignments.

However, as a student who wants to adhere to the utmost forms of integrity and credibility, it is incumbent upon you to put ethics before convenience and access. Therefore, we need to increase our adherence to ethical behaviors that protect the principles of ethical communication and creator content. Make it a habit of practicing ethical communication in the online environment by citing and sourcing the ideas of others. Doing this will become second nature, and you will avoid using the content of others without giving them credit.

Integrity and Credibility

We will discuss credibility in the following section of the chapter; however, it is worth mentioning here as we grapple with the practice of ethical communication in the online environment. When delivering digital presentations, one of the most important things you have is your integrity and credibility. Integrity and credibility are some things you practice in the delivery of your content and the composing of your content. As such, ethical research and planning go into your digital presentations and any messages you release to the public, both online and offline. Due to the nature of the digital sphere, once your integrity or credibility is compromised, your online reputation might be severely compromised. And remember, when communicating face-to-face, anyone can film you and release that content online, even if you do not know you are being filmed. Whether or not it is illegal in your state to record without your permission, your goal is to protect yourself from compromising your integrity and credibility. The best way to do this is to practice ethical communication in public at all times.

In the age of "cancel culture," where social media platforms like Twitter allow the public access to you, you are vulnerable to attacks due to the public's perceived or real view of your conduct. One of the best ways to protect your online reputation is to adhere to the standards of integrity and credibility in the content you publish and the messages you deliver both online and offline. Just like ethos (appeal to ethics), logos (appeal to logic) and pathos (appeal to emotion) are important in the delivery of face-to-face presentations, and they are important in the digital world, too. Observance of ethos, logos, and pathos will help you avoid the pitfalls of plagiarism in the digital environment.

Ethos, Logos and Pathos

Ethos, Logos and Pathos, which you will learn about throughout this text and as you learn to construct and deliver speeches, are integral to ethical public speaking practices. **Ethos,** appeal to ethics or character, will be diminished if you do not follow ethical practices in public speaking. **Credibility** is a speaker's trustworthiness or the audience's confidence in the information that the speaker is delivering. You can develop credibility throughout your speech, and often your reputation affords you a certain amount of credibility before you even deliver your speech. **Logos** appeals to logic, which means that you need to incorporate up-to-date, factual evidence into your speech. Inseminating misinformation or faulty data can destroy a speaker's character and, ultimately, the entire speech. Check and recheck your sources and data points. Make sure your data is factual, cross-referenced and sourced. **Pathos**, an appeal to emotions, requires that speakers use evidence, facts, and emotion to persuade and inform their audience. Speakers who use fear-mongering or appeal solely to the audience's emotions can incite and provoke unwarranted emotions in listeners. Therefore, speakers need to be aware of their words' power and the significance of the psychology of public speaking, even in the online environment. That is, do not rely so heavily on pathos that you cloud the audience's critical thinking—doing so is unethical.

Respect the Message

You should not mistake inclusivity with disagreement. If your position is different from someone else's, that does not mean you are not inclusive. You can share an oppositional point of view without being divisive or offensive. One way to do this is to use accurate and factual information that credible supporting materials can verify. Verify your supporting materials by checking the claims you intend to use in your speech, with at least two reputable sources.

Reputable sources include peer-reviewed academic journal articles and vetted news outlines with a history of fair and accurate reporting backed by scientific data. Additionally, when using images, music, songs or the like, it is especially important to follow copyright law for media used in your presentation. In the academic setting, fair use likely applies to how you will use media in your digital presentation as your content is not for commercial use or sale. While this chapter is not about copyright law specifically, it is prudent to take a quick look at a specific section of the United States Copyright Act:
Section 107 of the Copyright Act defines fair use as follows:

[T]he fair use of a copyrighted work, including such use by reproduction in copies or phonorecords or by any other means specified by that section, for purposes such as criticism, comment, news reporting, teaching (including multiple copies for classroom use), scholarship, or research, is not an infringement of copyright. In determining whether the use made of a work in any particular case is a fair use the factors to be considered shall include --

1. *the purpose and character of the use, including whether such use is of a commercial nature or is for nonprofit educational purposes;*
2. *the nature of the copyrighted work;*
3. *the amount and substantiality of the portion used in relation to the copyrighted work as a whole;*
4. *and the effect of the use upon the potential market for or value of the copyrighted work.*

Copyright law can be extensive and often confusing. Still, as we discussed in the section covering plagiarism, the best way to avoid issues is to source and cite, do not give presentations for commercial use that include the work of others unless you have written permission, and if your presentation is for commercial use or sale, consult a lawyer. For this chapter, you want to understand the basics of "fair use" as detailed above. The Digital Media Law Project cited in the reference section of this book is a great place to learn more (Digital Media Law Project, 2021).

Be Inclusive: Speaker, Message, Audience Cycle

Being inclusive can mean a lot of different things to various people. We could talk about using inclusive language or delivering a more accessible presentation or simply getting people involved in the presentation. Therefore, in the spirit of practicing effective communication, we want to define what we mean by *inclusive* in the context of this chapter.

Inclusive here represents what Dr. Sheena C. Howard terms the **Speaker, Message, Audience Cycle (or SMAC). SMAC** is best represented using the following as foundational guidelines:

- Reject content that normalizes racism, sexism, classism, homophobia, and other forms of bigotry.
- Avoid gender-specific and gender-binary language.
- Use material that can be seen, heard, and experienced by all listeners.

You can best incorporate this foundational approach in your presentation by viewing inclusivity as something that involves both attention to accessibility and inclusion around identity. The Speaker, Message, Audience Cycle (or SMAC) means that public speaking is about the relationship between a speaker, the message, and the audience, with ethics being at the center of all communication. Therefore, if you have audience members who cannot participate in this relationship, you open yourself up to excluding listeners. As the speaker, you are generally in a position of power in that you have a platform to deliver your message and can potentially influence the behavior and perspective of others. It would be best if you took that position and power seriously as well as responsibly, which is particularly true in the online environment, where you most likely have the ability to mute people at will and decide who gets to respond and who doesn't. Remember to respect all three of these elements and center ethics. These four elements are interdependent and need to work in tandem as you construct and deliver your speech.

As the speaker, you should aim to research, create, and deliver a presentation that does not exclude audience members who may not look, think, or act like you. In this active process, you must continually remind yourself of the interdependency of the four outlined elements. If you simply focus on the speaker, message, and audience without centering on ethics, then you open yourself up to engaging in exclusionary practices.

As previously mentioned, you can deliver controversial content or content with which your audience disagrees. Still, it does mean that the content should not elicit fear, harm, or judgment of others based on their identities. You can best stay clear of excluding audience members by delivering a fact-based and well-sourced speech, using references that are verifiable, credible, and relevant to your thesis and main points. In short, construct your speech and deliver your content using SMAC as your foundational approach.

Respect Your Audience

Respecting your audience requires two things: accountability and responsibility. One way to engage in ethical public speaking practices is to set responsible speech goals to maintain accountability for the consequences of your public communication. To be accountable means that you have considered your audience and how your presentation will affect others when preparing your speech and the delivery stage of the public speaking process. Considerations such as inclusive language, avoiding hate speech, assuming responsibility for raising social awareness, and employing respectful free speech are all responsible speech goals that you should consider (Millner and Price, 2016). In addition, you should consider how you appeal to the emotional fears and concerns of your audience (to the detriment of logical appeals), as well as how you use false or unsound arguments—**fallacies**—to support claims throughout your speech.

Appeals to Fear and Fallacies

Typically, in courses on persuasion or more advanced public speaking classes, you will learn about fallacies. However, it is important to briefly mention them here as they have implications for ethics in public speaking. Fallacies are misleading arguments or attacks on someone's character or personal traits without addressing disagreement with an argument. For example, a fallacy would look like this:

After Rob presents a compelling case for immigration reform, Jim asks the audience whether we should believe anything from a man who works for the border patrol, has several outstanding parking tickets, and is unattractive.

⑦ ETHICS IN ONLINE COMMUNICATION

Fallacies, although unethical, can be very effective in persuading audiences and winning arguments. Hopefully, you will continue to study communication and take advanced speech courses to further develop your knowledge around the different types of fallacies employed that often result in unethical public speaking practices. For now, be mindful of your approach to counter-arguments and persuasive speaking when writing and delivering your speeches.

According to Kaylene Williams (2012), in her article "*Improving fear appeal ethics*" in the *Journal of Academic and Business Ethics,* fear appeals are commonly used in many types of marketing communications (for example, the marketing of products, services, social causes, and ideas). Also, they are frequently used to get people to help themselves and generally effectively increase ad interest, involvement, recall, and persuasiveness. The literature conventionally agrees that more effective fear appeals result from higher fear-arousal followed by consequences and recommendations to reduce the negativity. Fear appeals have been criticized as unethical, manipulative, exploitative, eliciting negative and unhealthy responses from viewers, and exposing viewers to offensive images against their will (Williams, 2012), all unethical tactics people do use in public speaking. Thus, the ethical use of fear appeals can be improved, but public communicators should consider the often-blurry line between ethical and unethical fear appeals.

Kim Witte (1992, 1993, 1994), a prominent author in this area, defines fear appeals as "persuasive messages that arouse fear by depicting a personally relevant and significant threat, followed by a description of feasible recommendations for deterring the threat." Fear appeals work when you make the listeners very afraid and then show them how to reduce the fear by doing what you recommend (Williams, 2012).

As you move through this text, use the guidelines in this chapter to inform your research and delivery decisions. Starting with good habits, such as ethical listening, ethical research, productive public speaking qualities, and understanding the history of diverse approaches to communication, you develop "best practices" early on in your learning process. As we have noted in this chapter, employing these traits will benefit your personal, professional, and public life. Consider the following guidelines in incorporating accountability and responsibility into respecting your audience.

Topic selection

Understand that presentations are about your audience, not about you. Keeping your audience front and center is difficult to remember when you are presenting virtually, and your listeners aren't in the same room, or perhaps you can't even see them on your screen. Focus on framing your topic in terms of what you can provide the audience based on their needs and interests. One of the best ways to do this is to find out as much information as possible about who will be attending your speech, which might include age, title, positions, backgrounds and other variables that will help you position your speech and select the most appropriate topic based on who will be listening.

Identify with audience members

Establishing common ground is what Kenneth Burke termed the "new rhetoric." The process of identifying with your audience is powerful in engaging with listeners—whether you are there to persuade or inform. This process involves finding methods to connect with them in various ways, including but not limited to identity, issues, and perspective. For example, you may establish common ground by acknowledging that you and the listeners are in the same class, or go to the same school or work at the same place. In addition, you might acknowledge that you are all facing similar challenges overcoming the fear of public speaking. As a speaker, it is your job to engage in writing and delivering a speech that can establish common ground with the listeners.

Be honest

Never be dishonest about your intentions for speaking. Your speech should give a primer or preview statement up front, letting the audience know where your speech is headed and what you will cover in your presentation. Letting the audience know where you are going in your speech helps them feel engaged and follow along. After all, one of your goals as a speaker is to hold your audience's attention. This task can be more daunting in the online environment, where the listener has added distractions due to watching or engaging with you through a computer or cell phone.

Comply with the Americans with Disabilities Act (ADA)

As a speaker, you want to make sure your presentation is accessible to all types of listeners. The online environment allows us to use important technological tools that make it easier for people to engage. For example, you may have noticed that videos online often show the text of the speech or captioning at the bottom. Brands and marketers know that not everyone can listen to a speech; some people can only read the text of the video or audio. Thus, offering live captioning and subtitles is something you want your audience to have access to, where it is possible. Other tools and techniques you want to incorporate into your digital presentation are screen reader-friendly options, describing meaningful visuals verbally, incorporating silent pauses into your delivery and repeating questions to the audience instead of just making the audience read questions on a PowerPoint. These techniques will allow for the best experience possible for the greatest number of people.

Respect Yourself

As previously discussed in this chapter, credibility, integrity, accountability, and responsibility are important, both inside and outside the digital space. However, these characteristics that you need to embody can only be practiced if you have respect for yourself. When you respect yourself, you can then respect the identity of the audience without delivering disingenuous content. At times, you might find that you have a highly critical or oppositional audience. The best way to deliver a presentation to such an audience is to first begin with being credible, having integrity, and being accountable and responsible.

Critics can only be persuaded when you have incorporated logos into the construction and delivery of your speech, which entails incorporating ethics in terms of being a "good person speaking well" and pathos in believing and being passionate about your content.

Even critics can respect an oppositional viewpoint if they know the presenters have done their homework in terms of research (credibility) and display honesty (ethics) in their delivery. Thus, you respect yourself and your audience by maintaining your character and credibility when faced with an oppositional audience.

As you practice these guiding principles of avoiding plagiarism, respecting the message, inclusivity, and respecting your audience and yourself, it is important that you also include these in the process of listening. Listening as a speaker or presenter is just as important as listening to an audience member. As we conclude this chapter, we will focus on listening in the online environment and exploring how our foundational principles co-exist with listening.

Listening in the Online Environment

Listening in the online environment is just as important as speaking and creating content in the online environment. Listening also involves responding. The Five-Stage Model of Listening includes receiving, understanding, remembering, evaluating, and responding (DeVito, 2017). This model is a holistic cycle of listening that demonstrates a process that is relevant in face-to-face communication and online communication. You have ethical responsibilities as a listener.

Some early Greek and Roman philosophers —Aristotle, Socrates, and Plato—spoke extensively about morality and ethical principles. Just as there are ethical practices when it comes to speaking, there are also ethical practices for listening. In "Listening for Diversity" (2016), Sally Lehrman outlines four ethical ways news reporters can ethically listen as it relates to understanding the values of marginalized communities. She cites the following ways to better your listening by employing an ethical approach:

- Quiet your mind. Don't assume your definitions are the same as your sources. When coming across online messages or listening to digital presentations before responding or judging the message, try first to understand the sender of that message.

- Ask why? Look for the story behind the story. Listen for the reason behind the statement. It is easy online to read story headings or short Twitter posts and Tik Tok videos. Still, as a listener, you should read the entirety of an article or hear and see the entirety of a video to learn the context and details of a message. Choose integrity over convenience.

- Meet your sources where they are both literally and figuratively. You'll be able to hear better if you are in your source's comfort zone, not your own, which represents the concept of understanding in the Five stage model of listening. You must first try to understand before you evaluate and respond. Using this method will encourage people to be more forthcoming. In the online environment, understand that every controversial post or message you come across doesn't mean a response from you is required.

- Ask what your sources actually do, not just what they think or know. Many people in the online environment are not subject matter experts; they are just sharing their opinions. Before responding, recognize if the sender of a message is informed and educated on the subject matter or simply sharing an opinion that may not be informed, factual or in good faith. Just as you need to operate with integrity and credibility, many people in the online space are not operating from that standard. Be discerning enough to identify the difference.

Lehrman's ethical approach to listening shows us that audiences have a responsibility, which involves a process of listening beyond simply hearing or receiving soundbites. It is the listener's responsibility to acknowledge fairness and accuracy in the way we interpret and disseminate information, which cannot be done without practicing ethical listening as outlined above.

Think about how you can improve your communication skills online by simply incorporating these ethical listening guidelines into the digital space and in your interpersonal relationships that might be maintained using electronic tools. The combination of the guidelines laid out here can all be improved upon by being polite and attentive, avoiding prejudging the speaker, and ethically maintaining the free and open expression of ideas.

References:

Abbott, J., T., McDorman, D., Timmerman, & Lamberton. (2015). *Public Speaking and Democratic Participation: Speech, Deliberation, and Analysis in the Civic Realm.* Oxford University Press.

Copyleaks Technologies LTD. (2020, October 20). *The Impact of Social Media on Plagiarism.* Plagiarism Checker: AI Based Anti-Plagiarism Online. https://copyleaks.com/blog/the-impact-of-social-media-on-plagiarism/.

Devito, J. (2017). The Interpersonal Communication Book. Boston: Pearson Education.

Digitial Law Project (2021). Fair use. Retrieved from http://www.dmlp.org/legal-guide/fair-use

Gudykunst, W.B. & Y.Y. Kim, 1992). *Communicating with Strangers: An Approach to Intercultural Communication*, (2nd ed.) New York: McGraw Hill.

History of Public Speaking. (2016, May 26). Retrieved June 6, 2016, from Boundless website: https://www.boundless.com/communications

Lehrman, S. (2016). *Listening for Diversity.* Quill, 104(2), 38.

Lucas, S. E. (2001). *The Art of Public Speaking,* 7th ed. New York: McGraw-Hill.

McCabe, D. (n.d.). Statistics. Retrieved April 26, 2021, from https://www.academicintegrity.org/statistics/

McKay, B., & K. McKay(2011, January 26). Classical Rhetoric 101: The Five Canons of Rhetoric â€" Invention. Retrieved June 5, 2016, from the art of manliness website: http://www.artofmanliness.com/2011/01/26/ classical-rhetoric-101-the-five-canons-of-rhetoric-invention/

Millner, A., & R. Price, (2016, March). Ethics in Public Speaking. Retrieved June 7, 2016, from Public Speaking Project website: http://www.publicspeakingproject.org

O'Neill, M. T. (1980). Plagiarism: Writing Responsibly. *Business Communication Quarterly,* 43, 34-36.

Power, Mary R. and Camille Galvin, (1997) "The culture of speeches: Public speakin across cultures," *Culture Mandala: The Bulletin of the Centre for East-West Cultural and Economic Studies*: Vol. 2. Iss. 2, Article 2.

Schulz, P., & P Cobley,. (2013). *Theories and Models of Communication.* Berlin: De Gruyter Mouton.

Williams, K. (2012). Improving fear appeal ethics. *Journal of Academic and BusinesEthics*, 1-24. Retrieved June 05, 2016, from *http://www.aabri.com/manuscripts/11906.pdf* Witte, K. (1992). Putting the Fear Back into Fear Appeals: The Extended Parallel Process Model. *Communication Monographs,* 59(4), 329-349.

Witte, K. (1993). Message and Conceptual Confounds in Fear Appeals: The Role of Threat, Fear, and Efficacy. *The Southern Communication Journal,* 58(2), 147-156.

Witte, K. (1994). *Fear Control and Danger Control: A Test of the Extended Parallel Process Model (EPPM). Communication Monographs,* 61(2), 113-134.

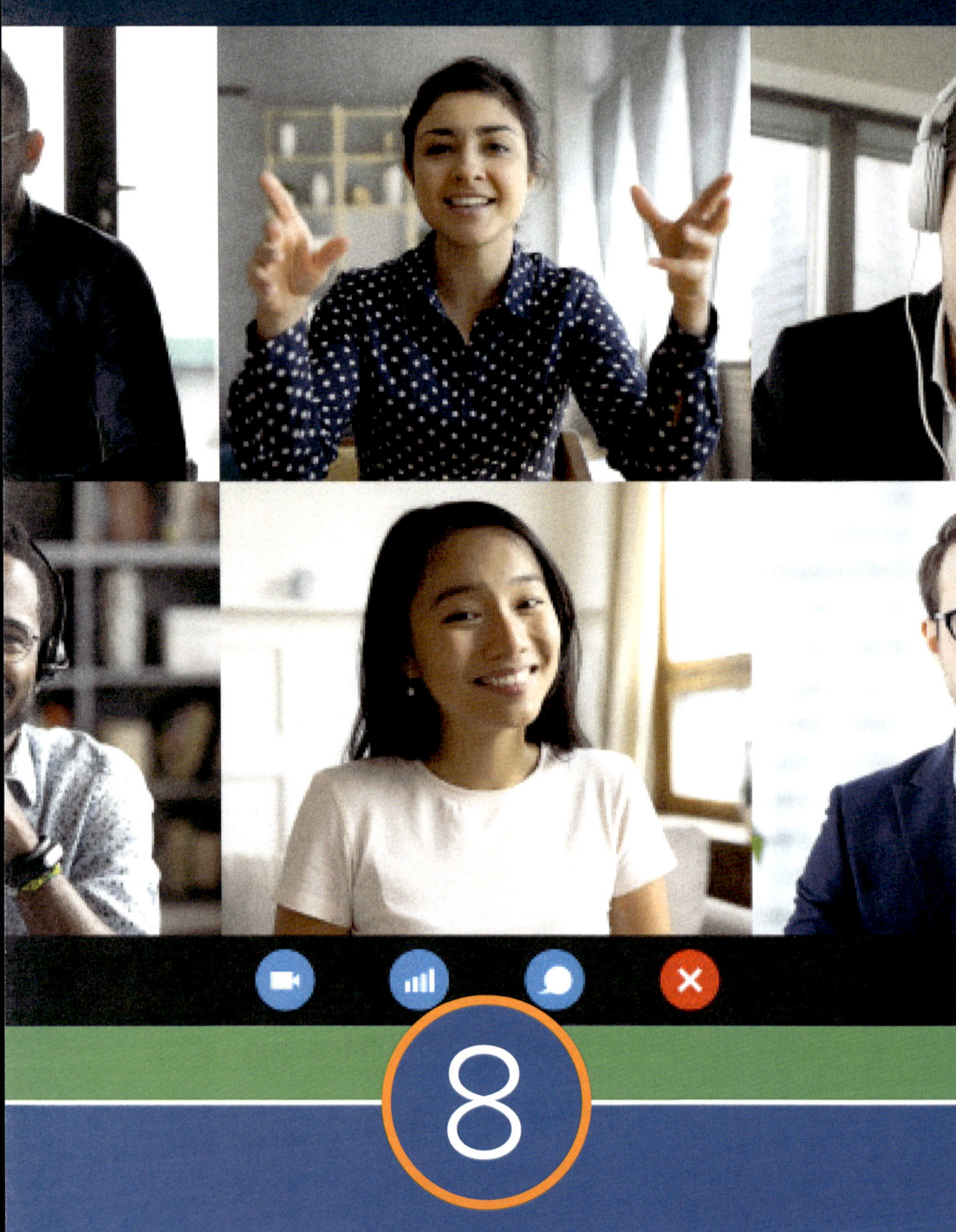

Delivery of Online Communication

Thomas S. Wright, PhD (Temple University)
Maxine Gesualdi, PhD (West Chester University)

While in-person job presentations and conferences will remain common, the convenience of online communication means it is here to stay. This chapter is not about whether one mode of communication, in-person or online, is better or worse. Instead, as a professional, you need to prepare for both modes of delivery. A fundamental similarity between in-person and online communication is that people's perceptions of you involve a combination of delivery factors: how you look and speak, how you comport yourself, and how well you adapt to the context of the situation. Understanding the unique dynamics of online communication is an essential part of your professional communication repertoire, whether you give a presentation, field a sales call or discuss possible career change. The particular dynamics of online communication include challenges such as finding the best location to set up a video feed, demonstrating your intent through nonverbal cues. This chapter focuses on the core aspects of effective and engaging online delivery, including your appearance, camera location, nonverbal communication, and paralanguage (or vocal emphasis). Your phone, tablet, or computer's camera is a window into your world, and you are letting others peek into it.

Appearance

In online communication, you often react to a person's appearance even before interacting with them. You see their face and the background in the camera shot before talking to them. In an online interview, you may be waiting, on-screen, for a few minutes before the interview begins. In a sales video call, you may have to wait for your potential client to finish paperwork or another meeting before they join you. If you are a student, your professor may see you for numerous class periods before you have the opportunity to speak one-on-one. It is common in online meetings for participants to be auto-muted upon entering the meeting or virtual room. That is, you are not allowed to speak but are you expected to be seen through your camera. It is crucial then to enter every online communication encounter knowing that as soon as you connect, you are "on stage." Your general appearance is a psychological shortcut to help us process information about people and express our own cultural and personal identity. Rightly or wrongly, *you can't recreate the first impression someone has of you.* This section provides specific tips and advice for an effective professional online appearance.

Clothing

You should always "dress up" to meet the communication context. That is, you should dress professionally and appropriately for any formal, professional virtual meeting. If there is ever any doubt, dress the way you would for a job interview. Whether it is an online conference, a training session mandated by human resources, or updating your superiors on a project; it is easier to take off your tie or remove a scarf than add one once you have started. There are some exceptions to these guidelines, such as a meeting among peer colleagues for informal updates or a virtual team-building event that is meant to be fun and casual. But, you should always dress for online meetings the way you would in your in-person office setting. If you do not have an in-person office setting, double-check the employee handbook to guide the dress code. Or ask a senior colleague about expectations. Also, think about the impression you want to make to the people you are meeting online.

As noted above, your appearance signals impressions about you to others. In online meetings, the way you dress can signal to others how serious you are about the given situation. For example, if you meet online with your manager to discuss your annual performance review, wearing a hoodie or a graphic tee may not be the best choice if the workplace expects business casual dress.

Because online platforms have certain visual constraints (video cameras do not process colors and patterns like the human eye), the following guidelines apply to most online meeting circumstances.

Best practices for dressing for online communication include:

- Know whether you will be sitting or standing and dress accordingly.
- Wear appropriate professional attire for the interaction. It is appropriate to ask the meeting organizer or another invited meeting participant if you are ever unsure what the person or organization expects.
- "Business casual" is appropriate for most online events, meetings, and discussions.
- Wear a solid color. Cameras and digital communication software often blur or distort patterns, which can be distracting.
- Avoid wearing solid whites, greens, and dark blacks. You do not want to get "green-screened." This is when a virtual background on your online meeting platform may distort your video feed, in some cases making you disappear.
- Wear an entire outfit. If you must stand up, you don't want an embarrassing incident where you look like you are only half-dressed.

Other Appearance Considerations

Similar to how you dress is how you prepare your personal appearance for professional interactions online. We all know that we do not always look the same online as we do in person. If you are unfamiliar with the way cameras may distort your appearance, and that is something that concerns you, you should practice using one of the many online meeting platforms or apps before your interaction. Similar to the advice above for dressing appropriately, tailor your appearance as if you are going to a job interview.

Best practices for personal appearance for online communication include:

- Style your hair so that it is not obscuring your face or eyes. Unlike in-person encounters, online, your face is the central focus and often takes up most of the computer screen.
- If you have facial hair, trim it so that it does not obscure your mouth.
- Apply some powder to minimize distracting shine.
- Avoid jewelry that has a lot of movement. Again, jewelry can be more distracting during online meetings because your face and torso are framed to a greater extent than in-person meetings.
- Check the lighting before your start and use a ring light if necessary.
- Position your camera lens to focus straight ahead or slightly down toward you. Think about positioning the camera around your hairline and tilted slightly down to see your entire face and upper body. This angle avoids people looking up your nose or just at half your face.
- `Make sure that the camera is not too close to you. It's best to see your shoulders and face with some room above your head.

If your job requires you to meet with clients regularly online, and your budget allows, consider investing in an external HD camera.

Background

While your upper body and face are the focal point, the background for your virtual interaction takes on heightened importance. Unlike in-person meetings where you go to their office, auditorium, or meeting room, you allow other people to see where you are located in online communication contexts. We have all become accustomed to working from our apartments, home, and dorm rooms. But the expectations for audience members differ based on your role, such as student or working professional. Much like how you dress and prepare your appearance, there are professional expectations for your visible background.

Best practices for preparing your background for online communication include:

- Blur your background or use a virtual background or green screen. Using virtual backgrounds is common practice to distinguish between personal and professional virtual space.

- If you allow others in the meeting to see your background, consider moving any "artifacts" (e.g., personal items such as posters, objects, or pictures). These can sometimes be distracting to the audience as they strain to see what is behind you.
- If you share a space with someone (e.g., roommate, spouse, co-worker), tell them the specific time of your meeting and ask them to refrain from inadvertently "joining" in the background.
- Alternately, style your background or the room you are in to highlight your personal flair or hint at your desire to be seen as an individual. A bookcase with selected books or memorabilia is almost always appropriate.
- Pets are cute, but not everyone finds them cute during a meeting. If possible, ensure that your pets are happy and secure in another location.

Location

Related to preparing your background is finding the best possible location for your online interaction. If you are conducting a paid webinar for clients or training new employees, the last thing you want is continuous distractions or a lost Wi-Fi signal. Just as important is that you feel comfortable and relaxed. If you are constantly worried about someone (like a meddling parent) or something (like construction) disrupting your sales call, it will be hard for you to be your best. In short, select a location that provides the best possible atmosphere for your virtual presentation.

Best practices for selecting a location for online communication include:

- Find a room where you are comfortable and familiar with the surroundings. You will be most relaxed and productive if you know nothing will take away from your meeting.
- Ensure there is little to no background noise that will interfere with your presenting or hearing the other participants.
- Make sure the lighting is appropriate. Natural light often provides the best look but never sit with a bright light or window behind you.
- Make sure you are close to the Wi-Fi router.
- If you have encountered problems in the past (e.g., construction, lost signal), let the other people in your meeting know when your meeting starts. Because we have all encountered problems and distractions, most people understand, especially when they know an issue may occur.

Nonverbal Communication

Nonverbal communication is any form of communication that does not include the spoken word. In online communication contexts, like meetings, presentations, and interviews, nonverbals play a prominent role in guiding how others interpret and understand the verbal aspects of communication. As noted previously, when online, your communication practices are framed and restricted by the screen. Because you have less space to present or interact with your audience, your nonverbals need to be more precise and controlled. Hence, they take on a greater communication value than they would during an in-person presentation or meeting. On the other hand, online communication does eliminate some forms of nonverbals such as olfactics (i.e., smell), gate or how your walk and move, stance (i.e., how you stand or position yourself), touch, and proxemics (i.e., use of space). This section provides specific best practices for using nonverbals, including kinesics (or body language), gestures, affect displays, and eye contact, as well as paralanguage. The fundamental rule for managing your nonverbals during a virtual meeting is that they complement and emphasize your verbal communication and not distract from it.

Kinesics

Kinesics, or body language, play an essential role in online presentations because, as previously noted, your upper body or torso is the camera's focus and framed by the computer monitor, tablet, or phone camera. While standing for virtual meetings is not unheard of, specifically for some conference presentations or product introductions, it is less common than sitting during online meetings. One specific issue with standing while presenting is audio quality and ambient sounds because few presenters wear computer-connecting microphones. If you are looking for a good guideline for how you will be seen or what it will be like watching or reviewing other presenters online, you will quickly note which nonverbal kinesic movements add to the presentation and those that detract.

The following guidelines assume you will be sitting for the duration of your virtual interaction.

Best practices for managing your kinesic communication include:
- Use a comfortable chair with good back support and consider a footrest.
- Sit back far enough from the camera so others in the meeting can see you gesture or use your hands.

- Adjust the height of your chair so you have easy access to the keyboard and you are looking into the camera.
- Relax your shoulders and straighten your back. You do not want to hunch over.
- Keep your elbows off the desk or table to prevent leaning on them or slouching.
- Remember you are in the frame for the camera, so avoid any excessive or distracting movements like swaying back and forth, side to side, slumping down, or stretching.
- Depending on the type of meeting, it is perfectly fine and professional to briefly turn off your camera to stand up, walk around, and stretch.

Gestures

Like an in-person presentation or interview, hand gestures are a critical tool for getting your point across, engaging your audience, and emphasizing essential points of your verbal remarks. Gestures are particularly helpful when discussing small numbers (i.e., using fingers to count), indicating increases or decreases in something (i.e., raising or lower hands, pointing up or down), giving instructions or directions, and showing comparisons. In addition, you can use gestures to emphasize a specific idea (e.g., pointing or clenching your hands or making a fist), demonstrate openness (e.g., displaying an open hand with palms out), or indicating excitement (e.g., moving your hands one in front of the other). You can also show interest by making a steeple with your fingers, frame an idea with a "hand box," or clapping. You can also use evaluative gestures such as a thumbs up or down, hugging yourself, or putting your hand on your heart.

A good rule of thumb is to mimic or mirror the gestures you would use in an everyday conversation or traditional in-person presentation within the camera frame.

Best practices for managing your gesture for online communication include:
- Sit in a position where you can use your hands, and they are easily seen.
- Rest hands on the table in front of you with most of your forearms on the desk or table. Alternately, you can rest your hands on your keyboard if you can quickly gesture as needed.
- Keep your gestures at a moderate distance from the camera but in front of your body. In short, you do not want your hands too close to the camera. They will take up the screen and obscure your face.
- Gesture with purpose and deliberately. That is, your gestures should have a specific purpose and be done more slowly because cameras tend to exaggerate quick movements.
- Avoid fiddling with your hands or objects. While it may not seem distracting to you, others are often hyper-aware of even tiny movements on screen.
- Clapping and snapping can show excitement or approval but should not be overused or done in an exaggerated manner. Your microphone is sensitive to loud, distinct sounds.
- Do not cross your arms. While it may seem harmless, crossed arms are a universal symbol of hostility or boredom.

Affect Displays and Eye Contact

Affect displays are facial expressions used to convey emotion. Affect displays are particularly important to regulate and monitor during online communication because your face is the focal point of the interaction. As noted previously, center your face on the screen. It provides the most salient nonverbal cues for the other person to understand what you are saying in an interaction. For example, to demonstrate interest and enthusiasm in an employment interview, we often smile slightly more, and our eyes are open wider. When listening to a customer's question, a salesperson will nod along to demonstrate understanding. During a meeting with your professor, if you are confused or have difficulty following along, you might slightly tilt your head and scrunch your eyes. Eye contact is a specific type of affect display and one of the most sighted ways to interpret a person's emotions. The most obvious example is interest, looking at the person while speaking, and disinterest, looking away or being inattentive.

Affect displays are natural and mainly occur without conscious thought. However, you need to monitor your affect displays and eye contact in professional settings to ensure you are sending the intended message.

Best practices for managing your affect displays for online communication include:

- Facial expressions should complement and emphasize your verbal message. For example, you can smile, nod, or frown.
- Avoid touching your face and your hair. Primarily, you may mess up your makeup or hair, but you may also be signaling impatience or nervousness.
- Pay attention to how others use affect displays to convey meaning and emotion. While you are the presenter, you should note how others respond (i.e., they may be confused and need clarification or may want to interject a comment).

Best practices for managing eye contact for online communication include:

- The best way to connect with your audience is through eye contact. We have a natural tendency to be more engaged and interested when someone makes sustained eye contact.
- Look at the webcam, not the computer screen. Making consistent eye contact may take some practice, but you do not want to look away from others regularly as this could create disengagement with others in the online setting.
- Position the camera, so you are looking directly into it or very slightly up. If necessary, prop your tablet, laptop, or phone on a small box or some books.
- When a meeting has multiple participants, switch your platform or app from gallery to speaker mode. You then avoid dropping eye contact to look around the screen for the speaker.

Paralanguage (The Voice)

Paralanguage is *how* something is said rather than the specific words used. Characteristics of paralanguage include pitch, rhythm, tempo, and volume. Because we cannot speak without using paralanguage, every word transforms when spoken. Notice how strange you sound when you try to speak with no inflection, at a set volume and constant rate. Paralanguage gives you a dynamic range of voice by changing your tone and pitch, engaging your audience, and emphasizing specific ideas or words. In everyday conversation, we use our voice to bring communication to life. Take, for example, the word "wow." I may slowly pronounce the word, drawing it out, slightly raising my voice, "woooo OOOWWW," indicating growing interest and excitement. I may sarcastically say it quickly and with no pitch, as in "wow." Because online communication lacks or constrains some of the nonverbal cues found in in-person communication, paralanguage takes on added importance. In general, you should pay attention to *how* you are saying something as much as *what* you are saying.

Best practices for managing paralanguage during online communication include:

- Avoid being monotone. Your online paralinguistics should mimic those you use in everyday interactions. Sales meetings, staff meetings, webinars, and recruiting events don't have to be boring. Use your personality and paralinguistics to keep everyone interested.
- Emphasize keywords and memorable phrases using vocal inflection, pitch, pauses, and tone.
- Focus on clarity. One difference between everyday conversation and professional interactions is that you need to speak more clearly and at a slower pace when communicating online.
- Be articulate and do not mumble. Practice saying any unfamiliar words before your meeting.
- Complete your thoughts. Do not let your voice trail off at the end of sentences.
- Moderate and vary the volume and rate of your voice for emphasis and engagement.
- Do not read from a prepared text.

Vocal Segregates

A specific type of paralanguage is vocal segregates. As the term implies, vocal segregates are breaks or pauses in verbal communication often used to regulate the flow of information or emphasize critical pieces of information. Vocal segregates include pauses, ahs, ums, and other nonfluencies (e.g., yeah, you know, like, etc.). In professional presentations, nonfluencies are sometimes interpreted as a lack of preparation or knowledge about a topic. However, because nonfluencies are common in nonprofessional situations, they may be seen as a sign of authenticity or genuineness. In other words, no one expects you to be perfect, but they do expect you to be well-practiced and prepared. This is true in training webinars, job interviews, presentations, or making remarks for a virtual awards ceremony.

Best practices for using vocal segregates during online communication include:

- It is okay to pause. You do not have to fill in every vocal stoppage with a sound or word. Pauses allow the audience to process information and indicate topic changes.

- Avoid using too many segregates because they may distract your audience, or they may lose interest.

- Record yourself when practicing so you can hear how often you use segregates. Do not be afraid to replace segregates with pauses.

- Be cautious with long pauses because, in an online setting, other participants may assume there is a technical problem.

Deliberating on Delivery for Online Communication

As outlined in this chapter, people's perceptions of you involve a combination of delivery factors: how you look and speak, how you comport yourself, and how well you adapt to the context of the situation. To convey your message, you need to think beyond the words you want to say. You need to consider your appearance, camera shot and background, location, nonverbals, and paralanguage. It may seem like a lot of moving parts to consider. And it is! Professional communication takes thought and practice. Not everyone can communicate well naturally. In fact, very few people can! Good communicators take the time to think not only about what they will say but how they will say it. Adding the variables from online communication to the mix requires an even more deliberate focus on professionalism than in-person communication. Knowing the limitations and benefits of online communication will help you adapt your personal style to this medium. And, putting into practice the tips from this chapter will help you authentically communicate with purpose and polish.

Anxiety and Apprehension for Virtual Presentations

Dr. Tracey Quigley Holden
University of Delaware

One of the most common feelings associated with giving presentations is anxiety - sometimes called stage fright, nerves, or even a type of phobia. Yet there are some people who are quite comfortable presenting to large audiences, but who feel anxious at a party, in meetings, or in one-on-one situations like interviews. Scholars in communication are well aware of this phenomenon and in research have found that people experience anxiety in many communicative situations, not just giving presentations to an audience. More than forty years ago, Dr. James McCroskey labelled this common feeling "communication apprehension" and began developing measurements and scales for assessing the anxiety felt in many communication situations (McCroskey, 1970). But thousands of years ago, teachers of communication and practitioners of presentation had been discussing how to manage stage fright and feelings of anxiety associated with communication. In this chapter you will learn about what "communication apprehension" is and how to manage it in ways that help you communicate more effectively, no matter how you are feeling in the moment. "Feel the Fear and Do It Anyway" was the title of a popular book in 1987 which quickly showed up on bumper stickers, posters and as a motivational quote for many people. More practically, it can be a personal mantra and a little extra push for facing and managing communication apprehension.

Glossophobia, Social Phobia, and Social Anxiety Disorder

In 2013, Google marketed a tablet as a research and education tool for K-12 students. In its advertising, it showed a middle school boy searching for "glossophobia", which Google defined as the fear of public speaking. While that is accurate, many if not most people experience feelings of anxiety and stress when asked to give any kind of presentation to an audience, as you read earlier. Those feelings are uncomfortable, but not to the point of causing people to avoid giving presentations entirely.

Glossophobia and social phobia are types of social anxiety disorder, a recognized mental health condition. The Mayo Clinic defines social anxiety disorder to include "fear, anxiety and avoidance that interferes with your daily routine, work, school or other activities" (Mayo Clinic, 2017). These conditions can contribute to, but are distinguishable from the communication apprehension described earlier. Social anxiety disorder is characterized by intense and persistent feelings of fear of humiliation, judgment, failure, and anxiety that seem uncontrollable. They can cause people suffering from them to avoid a wide range of social situations, even when such avoidance is personally or professionally costly. It is estimated that about 7% of the U.S. population suffers from a social anxiety disorder (National Institute of Health, 2017).

Glossophobia is a performance-related anxiety. People with performance anxiety may not have difficulty in social situations, but instead feel anxious when called on to give a digital presentation, speak in class or on Zoom, or any other forms of performance, such as dancing or playing music, sports competitions, or taking a test. There are very effective therapeutic and medical treatments for social anxiety disorder and for performance anxiety.

Knowing about 7% of people have to deal with social anxiety, let's consider that in the context of a typical communication class of 20-30 students, about 2 people might be affected with social anxiety in some form, which may add to feeling anxious about presenting. For nearly all students, the anxiety and stress they feel before presenting is common, manageable communication apprehension. That's what made the Google ad so effective; it showed that good information and preparation could reduce anxiety related to many forms of presenting to an audience. The underlying skills transfer between the widely different situations calling for communication. Even students with social anxiety can use the techniques here to reduce their anxiety about presenting.

Anxiety in a Digital World

Finding ways to deal with our apprehension effectively and positively is helpful in managing our anxiety about our public presentations, whether they are digital, in person, or a hybrid such as Zoom or Skype. It's also important to remember that our online presence can be seen as an opportunity to practice presenting our best selves. Think about how you use digital technology to connect with others. If you Snapchat with a friend, make a TikTok or YouTube video or update your LinkedIn profile with a video resumé, you can give a digital presentation – you already have! It may feel different to deliver a planned presentation, but the skills are the same – and the audience for your presentation is more likely to be positive than the trolls on TikTok! Knowing that you already use the skills you need for effective presentations in all of your daily interactions, whether they are in person or digital, could help you manage any apprehension you might feel.

The Betrayal and Benefit of Biology

In order to understand and manage your communication apprehension, it helps to know something about stress, human biology and the production of fear. Neuroscience and biology tell us there is a predictable, physical response to all forms of stress, preparing your body and brain to take action. Knowing what that is and how it works is what the next section is all about.

It is well known that the human brain and body are wired to respond to stress of any kind with a "fight or flight" response. In the early twentieth century, Walter Cannon identified the response and began research on the physiological causes and effects in humans. There are two parts to the response, each produced by different areas of your brain.

When we experience stress of any kind, our brains and bodies produce a response geared to help us either fight or flee from the situation. One concept which helps us understand brain function is the "triune brain" (Maclean, 1990) or three general brain parts with specific functions. While this is widely acknowledged to be a gross oversimplification of brain structures, it does give us a way to conceptualize brain activity. So the brain stem and cerebellum handle automatic, reflexive behavior – basically the things you should not spend time thinking about, like breathing and keeping your heart beating. This is sometimes called the reptilian or "lizard brain", as it is arguably the oldest part of our brains, essential to life, but lacks the ability to reason. The limbic system, including the amygdala, handles emotional responses but at the gut level – it feels, but does not think. The cerebrum and neocortex form the larger part of your brain, and they handle memories, planning, and thinking in general. So in the FIRST response to stress or strong emotions, your "lizard brain" signals the body to produce extra quantities of several hormones, including adrenaline and cortisol. Your limbic system contributes intense feeling and heightened awareness. Adrenaline heightens the muscular response and glucose available for immediate action, while cortisol suppresses the immune system and converts fatty acids to energy. The lizard brain and limbic system are boosting all your available systems to give you maximum energy. Unfortunately, this hormonal and emotional activity tends to have some unpleasant side effects, such as increased heart rate, a feeling of flushed skin, cold hands and feet, the feeling of your throat constricting, butterflies in the stomach, shaking or trembling of your muscles, and others. The side effects and what is noticed in a stress response vary from person to person, but the physiology is almost identical.

Your brain perceives a need for energy, and enthusiastically dumps hormones into your system to provide it. But your lizard brain, the part of your brain that manages these responses, doesn't have rational thought capabilities - it doesn't care if you are seeing a saber toothed tiger or giving a two minute presentation. Instead, it works on a stimulus-response basis. Got stress? Get energy! Your lizard brain and limbic system together can act a like a toddler with a box of cookies and no adult supervision, grabbing as much as they can from the box as fast as they can. More, more, more! Why have one when you can have them all? The result is a system overload and overreaction driven by physical and emotional reactions. This is the betrayal of our biology - our lizard brains and limbic systems have no ability to think. When your thinking brain, the neo-cortex, finally kicks in, it can help to assess and manage the thoughtless responses of your lizard and limbic systems. A key part of the thinking brain's job is to identify and label – give words to – our physical and emotional responses. This is the SECOND response, and it can lag well behind the first response. Your thinking brain starts analyzing the situation, using language to describe and label the key pieces. Your thinking brain can tell the toddler to have one cookie, notices that there is NO saber toothed tiger in the area, and recognizes that the audience for your presentation is actually pretty harmless. That's the benefit of biology! If you were actually in danger, your lizard brain would have given you a quick response to save your skin. If there is no imminent danger, your thinking brain can usually take over, label the situation, and use the energy to produce an appropriate response.

So from the beginning, it is important to understand that the physical and emotional feelings you may have are driven by your brain and body trying to give you energy to cope with perceived stress. *The physiology is the same, no matter what kind of stress you are experiencing.* This is where our thinking brain and our use of language can be a huge benefit. In our SECOND response, when we think, we can assess the situation accurately and manage our physical and emotional response effectively. A key part of this process is to recognize the feelings for what they are — a response to stress, the creation of extra energy - and label them in ways that help us act effectively. Thinking is done with language. We cannot think about something until we name it, so we can use naming to help us manage the response.

Imagine for a moment that you are getting ready to go to a party. You're within minutes of departing, and everything is going well. You're rushing just a bit to be ready on time. You know that good friends will be there, the party is well planned with fun things to do, and even the weather is cooperating. As you grab your keys and head for the door, how do you feel?

Here's another scenario - you are getting ready to go take an exam. You've studied hard, but you're just not sure you really understand all the material. A big part of your grade depends on this test, and a lot of your classmates have been texting about how hard they're studying — some have been up all night. You got some sleep, you've had a good breakfast and an extra cup of coffee, and you think you're ready. As you grab your keys and head for the door, how do you feel?

Most likely for the first scenario, your imagined feeling excited, happy, and eager to get to the party. In the second situation, you probably imagined feeling anxious, stressed, and reluctant to go take the test.

Guess what? Your brain and body are responding to each of these stress situations with extra adrenaline and emotional intensity. The difference is that in the first scenario, your mind is labeling those responses and feelings with words like "happy" "excited" and "anticipation". In the second, your mind is grabbing different labels like "anxious" "stressed" and "worried". You are interpreting the same physical and emotional responses in your brain and body differently. In both situations, your brain and body are responding to stress with the same physiological actions, while your mind is applying different words.

If you understand that the physiological response is just energy, and that you can choose how to label it, you are well on your way to being able to manage your communication apprehension! The next section will discuss effective techniques for relabeling, reducing, managing, and even benefitting from the communication apprehension you experience.

Managing Communication Apprehension

Once you understand the biology of apprehension, you are in a much better position to get your thinking brain in gear and able to mitigate the intense response of the lizard brain and limbic system. In addition to managing your involuntary brain and body responses, there are a variety of exercises and techniques that will help you boost your confidence and focus. There are several things you can do to manage communication apprehension, starting well before your actual presentation.

Prepare (Don't Procrastinate)

Normally, you have some time to prepare before you have to give your presentations. The single most effective thing you can do to reduce your communication apprehension is to prepare your presentation thoroughly, and well ahead of the due date. Taking the time to really know and understand the topic you will be speaking about, finding and organizing high quality information, and planning your presentation carefully for both the audience and the time available are all essential to giving an excellent presentation. As a bonus, every aspect of preparation also reduces communication apprehension. The more familiar and comfortable you are with your material and your plan for presentation, the more confident and less apprehensive you will feel. Ideally, you would know the content of your presentation so well that delivering your message is almost effortless – instead, you can focus on the response from the audience and adapting your message in the moment. When it comes to effective presentation, procrastination is one of your worst enemies. Procrastination leads to stress, which can amplify your feelings of apprehension. Even if you feel that some spontaneity or inspiration is lost in the process, the advantages of thorough preparation of your materials far outweigh the disadvantages of leaving preparations until too late.

Practice

Once you have the content and organizational plan for your presentation, practice is crucial. Moving from the written pages or notecards you have prepared to effective delivery to an online or in person audience takes practice, if only because what is written down does not always sound right when spoken aloud. Multiple rehearsals of your presentation will help you recognize the places where it flows smoothly or hits bumps, where you are comfortable with the material or need to get more familar, and identify the spots that need polishing or where a note or reminder would help. As a management practice for communication apprehension, an additional benefit of multiple rehearsals is desensitization. Systematic desensitization is a psychological technique used for many fears and phobias. Exposure to a smaller level of the stimulus that provokes fear or anxiety in a controlled situation helps you to reduce your stress response. Over time your brain learns that stimulus X does not pose a significant threat, and your stress response decreases. When you practice giving your presentation, especially if you either imagine your audience there or actually have someone watch you, you are simulating the stress of the actual presentation but at a reduced level. By engaging in the behavior that your brain perceives as stressful in an environment which is more comfortable for you, you become 'desensitized' to the situation. The more often you practice, the more your brain recognizes the situational cues correctly and gives you just the energy you need, instead of going to full alert.

Breathe

An important technique you can use to de-stress is so simple and quiet, it can be done anywhere – just breathe. Oxygen is a great antidote to anxiety. Your body is ready to respond to any perceived threat with fight or flight, and part of that reaction is an increased heart rate and faster breathing. Those shallow, quick breaths cut down on the oxygen available in your system and heighten your feeling of tension. Taking a deliberately slow, deep breath, holding it for a second or two, and releasing it slowly, helps your body reset itself, and to know that it is not immediately threatened. That deep breath actually uses some of the energy being used to speed up your systems, and using the energy acts as a counter to the adrenaline boost in the system. Adding oxygen to the mix also tells your brain and body that you are not at immediate risk. Taking a deep breath also gives your thinking brain time to take a little more control of the situation. It's a little like pushing a reset button. Once you've taken a good deep breath (or two) you can reassess your situation and take action to help your performance.

Use Your Body (Release, Redirect, Reframe)

When we experience stress, it's not unlikely that someone will tell us to "Keep Calm and Carry On" – borrowed from the famous British World War II poster. It's worth knowing that those posters were never distributed to the British people. They were kept in storage, to be used only in the worst case scenario of a German invasion. The phrase was intended to help Britons endure hardship and extreme circumstances which might go on for a long time. "Keep Calm and Carry On" may sound like an effective way to manage unavoidable stress or anxiety, but it is very difficult to do in the moment. When your brain and body are in "fight or flight" stress response mode, calming down is an impractical goal. Instead, realizing that the physical response to stress creates an abundance of energy in the human body, you can find ways to release or redirect that energy. You can also use your body to create a physiological response that will help you perform better.

The first technique is to release some of the extra energy you have. The easiest way to release it is to burn it off! If you have a choice between taking a few flights of stairs or taking the elevator, take the stairs. If you can walk around a bit, do so. If you have to stay in one place, squeeze your hands into fists and open them a few times, or tap your feet on the floor. Shrug your shoulders up and down. Any way you feel comfortable moving in a controlled way, move. As you burn off the energy, your sense of intensity and anxiety will diminish as well.

Releasing your extra energy should still leave you with more than you need to give your presentation. This is where the redirection of your energy can help you. Elite athletes, musicians, and other creative people spend hours practicing their skills, but many of them also use visualization for specific elements of their performance. An active visualization helps redirect your energy into creating the actions you need to perform. Tennis players will visualize every motion of a perfect serve, golfers a perfect swing, musicians see themselves perfectly producing every note. Redirecting your energy through visualization teaches you what you need to do to perform successfully – it's a form of mental rehearsal of the physical performance. A short visualization of yourself successfully giving your presentation channels your energy into reproducing that success. As you visualize your movements, gestures, and "see" yourself giving a great speech, you are simultaneously teaching your body and brain how to recreate it in real performance. Another visualization technique is called the Bubble. For the Bubble, you imagine yourself inside a lovely bubble, which smells and feels like your favorite place in the world. While in your bubble, you start your presentation and the bubble expands to include all of your audience members. Giving your speech is effortless! After you conclude, your bubble shrinks down to just enclose your body, and you can float happily along through your day. The Bubble also redirects your energy into your audience connection and your message, and away from your reactive state of apprehension.

The final technique for managing communication apprehension actually does quite a bit more than just help with a presentation. Dr. Amy Cuddy at Harvard Business School conducted research on the effect of particular physical positions of the body for people giving short presentations. The study showed that people who adopted "high power poses" for periods of two and five minutes prior to their presentation were evaluated more positively and their presentations were given better ratings than people who adopted "low power poses" for the same periods of time (Cuddy, Wilmuth and Carney, 2012). Cuddy's research (and her TED talk) explain that our senses of confidence and competence are affected by the way we hold our bodies. High power poses are expansive and take up

more space; they increase feelings of dominance, action, risk-taking and increase pain tolerance. High power poses also reduce stress and anxiety – and of course we know that reducing stress and anxiety is the key to managing communication apprehension! One way to use this research is to simply hold a power pose for a few minutes, shortly before your give your presentations. The high power poses Cuddy used in her research are pictured here.

But more than just boosting confidence and reducin rame how we see ourselves in the world, as more competent and powerful than we might feel in those moments before giving a speech. Competent, powerful, action oriented people still feel anxiety and apprehension, but they choose to "feel the fear and do it anyway."

Use Your Thinking Brain (Relabel and Rename)

Even with thorough preparation and practice, you are likely to still feel some communication apprehension. As discussed earlier, this is a normal physiological and emotional response of your brain and body to any form of stress. You can still use your "thinking brain" to help you manage both your physical responses and the emotional feelings of stress. First, new research from Harvard Business School (Brooks, 2014) shows that recognizing the emotional feelings of stress and relabeling them more positively can "flip the switch" of your experience. Excitement is the emotional twin of apprehension. Both involve some uncertainty in anticipation of action, but our labels are different. The technique used at Harvard is simple - as you notice the feeling of apprehension, you say out loud, "I am excited!" or "Get excited!" Instead of perceiving the situation as a threat, you relabel your perception to see it as an opportunity. That perceptual switch helps you relabel your feelings, switching from apprehension to excitement. The bonus of relabeling is that it also improves performance. Participants in the research who relabeled with "I am excited!" or "Get excited!" were scored higher by observers. When study participants were tasked with giving a speech, the participants who said "I'm excited!" out loud scored higher on persuasiveness, persistence, competence, and confidence. Those are pretty positive qualities for any presenter!

If switching from apprehension to excitement seems a bit of a stretch, or if you want an added boost for your performance overall, you can rename your physical responses. The technique is similar to relabeling, but focuses on identifying and directing the physical responses of your body as energy for your performance. The first act of our thinking brain is to find words for the feelings produced by the reptilian and limbic systems. Our words, especially those used for responses associated with emotions, have both denotative and connotative meanings. The denotative meanings are the dictionary definitions, the core meaning of the words. The connotative meanings are the additional interpretations imposed on the word by our experiences. For example, we all agree that "cat" has a denotative meaning of four-legged mammal of the feline species. For someone who loves cats, "cat" carries many other positive connotations – love, warmth, pleasure, purring. For a person who is not so fond of cats, "cat" might carry connotations of scratching, hissing, witches and bad luck. Neither connotation is wrong, but they are definitely different!! Thus the words we use to name something bring their own connotations along with the core meanings. Recall our discussion of the lizard brain's contribution of adrenaline and cortisol. Both hormones act to maximize the energy available to you and the speed of your responses. By naming the physiological response as energy, your thinking brain helps to diminish the emotional aspect of the response and the connotations that are associated with whatever words you might have named those emotions. Energy is what we all need to accomplish the tasks on our to-do lists. Identifying and renaming your physical response as energy helps you direct that energy toward your presentation.

These techniques can be used separately or together. Relabeling and renaming the physical and emotional response to stress does take some thinking effort, and a certain level of awareness of your own responses to stress. For some people, it is easier to relabel the emotional response; for others, renaming the physical response as energy is easier. There is no right or wrong way to use these techniques – try both and see what works for you!

Conclusion

In this chapter, we have discussed the challenge of communication apprehension, how the brain and body produce it and how our brains and bodies can help us manage and reduce it. It's important to remember that nearly every presenter experiences some form of communication apprehension. Recognizing the effects of communication apprehension from a physiological perspective is the key to effective management. Preparation and practice can reduce anxiety before your presentation. Relabeling and renaming techniques can be used in the moment of your presentation. Releasing, redirecting and reframing before, during, and after your presentation can shape your experience and your response in positive ways. Communication apprehension isn't going away, but it doesn't have to keep you from presenting your point of view!

References

Brooks, A. W. (2014). Get excited: Reappraising pre-performance anxiety as excitement. Journal of Experimental Psychology: General, 143(3), 1144–1158. https://doi.org/10.1037/a0035325

Cannon, W. B. (1932). The wisdom of the body. Kegan.

Cuddy, A. (n.d.). Your body language may shape who you are. Amy Cuddy: Your body language may shape who you are | TED Talk. Retrieved from https://www.ted.com/talks/amy_cuddy_your_body_language_may_shape_who_you_are

Cuddy, A. et al., (2012) "The Benefit of Power Posing Before a High-Stakes Social Evaluation." Harvard Busines School Working Paper, No. 13-027

Dobrean, A., and Paserelu, C-R. (2016). Impact of Social Media on Social Anxiety: A Systematic Review. In New Developments in Anxiety Disorders, eds. Federico Durbano and Barbara Marchesi (p. np). IntechOpen.

Jeffers, S. (1987). Feel the fear and do it anyway. Random House.

MacLean, P. D. (1990). The Triune Brain in evolution: Role in paleocerebral functions. Plenum.

Mayo Clinic. (2017, March). Social Anxiety Disorder. Retrieved from Mayo Clinic: http://www.mayoclinic.org/diseases-conditions/social-anxiety-disorder/basics/symptoms/con-20032524

McCroskey, J. C. (1970). "Measures of Communication-Bound Anxiety." Speech Monographs, 37(4), 269.

U.S. Department of Health and Human Services. (n.d.). Social anxiety disorder: More than just shyness. National Institute of Mental Health. Retrieved from https://www.nimh.nih.gov/health/publications/social-anxiety-disorder-more-than-just-shyness

O'Day, E, and Heimberg, R. (2021). Social media use, social anxiety, and loneliness: A systematic review. Computers in Human Behavior Reports, 1-13.

10

Visual Aids for Virtual Presentations

Karen Brager
Rowan University

What are visual aids, and why do we use them? A visual aid can be a variety of things. It can be a physical object such as a piece of fruit; it can be a demonstration showing yoga poses, or it may be a slide show using presentation software such as Microsoft's PowerPoint. For our purposes, we will discuss the presentation software approach to the visual aid. This type of aid can be useful whether you are speaking in person or virtually. This chapter will touch base briefly about other types of aids but will focus mainly on the presentation software aid.

Remember that you and your visual aid are partners. You each have your role; however, you, as the presenter, are the star of the show. The visual aid is your sidekick to help clarify and visualize your ideas and information, as needed. Your presentation should be able to "stand-alone" if your visual aid became unavailable for any reason. Dobrin et. al share four possible purposes that visual aids should serve in their text, *Technical Communication in the Twenty-First Century* (2nd ed.). They are to explain, emphasize, interest, and guide. Let's review the four.

- Visual aids can be the key to *explaining* ideas and concepts that are not easy to understand.
- They can also *emphasize* a key point or give a visual representation.
- Visual aids can *interest* your audience—if executed properly. They may get the audience curious, help them connect on a more emotional level, or help the audience focus on something other than you, the speaker (which helps to put you at ease if you are nervous).

Lastly, the visual aid can help *guide* the audience with your presentation's progress. A presentation should have a preview slide toward the beginning, giving the main ideas that will be covered. The audience will take note and keep track of where you are in the presentation. Such a slide helps to keep them focused, and it often helps keep you, the speaker, focused.

Types of visual aids

There are many types of visuals that persons can use to aid their presentation, whether in person or virtually. For our purposes here, we will split them into two categories, physical and digital. Physical aids can include the following: the speaker physically demonstrating a skill such as a yoga pose or making origami; physical objects such as a skateboard or a shoe, this can include a scale model as well, perhaps a battleship or car model; flip charts or a white/chalkboard; and handouts (if in person) or files (if virtual), which are not recommended for use during your presentation as they could distract your audience. Save handouts or file links for the end.

The digital aids are in the form of media and presentation software. Media can be film or TV clips, YouTube videos, or animated images. The presentation software used will vary. One of the most common programs used is Microsoft's PowerPoint, especially in corporate settings. You can embed media clips within the presentation, but you can also choose to share separately with your audience, depending on the situation and equipment.

Your presentation most likely will occur in one of three different situations. In-person, on a video conferencing platform such as Zoom or Google Meet, or as a pre-recorded presentation. There will always be differences, but the overarching ideas shared in this chapter can be applied to all.

Presentation Preparation

Before delving deeper into the topic of visual aids, *let's discuss the steps of preparing your presentation.* Your presentation is first and foremost filled with content. The first step is to create some type of thesis statement. A thesis statement tells the reader what the general and specific purposes of your presentation are. An example: *To inform my audience about the changes in major league baseball in 2021, including changes to the baseball, altering the rules of strategy and umpire review announcements.*
A strong and detailed thesis statement will help guide you in crafting your presentation. The content will vary in definitions, examples, statistics, and testimony. Each speech should have an introduction, body, and conclusion along with the thesis statement. Write

your presentation in a document or an outline using full sentences, which creates your presentation, and you will create notes from the full document.

At this stage of the process, you aren't thinking about your visual aid. While researching your presentation, you should note any diagrams, illustrations, short media clips, and so forth that you may want to include. Write down the location of the items for future reference. Once this process is complete, then it is time to prepare for your visual aid. And keep that list handy.

Your content may vary, depending on the subject matter and the occasion. If you are an art historian discussing the Sistine Chapel, you may rely mostly on images, but if you are an insurance professional, your talk most likely will have a good number of graphs and charts. The bulk of your talk will be filled with examples, statistics, and testimony. These three types of supporting materials help your audience to understand your subject matter.

- Examples help you to illustrate ideas and concepts.
- Statistics provide numerical data.
- Testimony is from someone who has experience in the topic, whether it be personal or professional.

Below are examples of slides that aid a presentation's examples, statistics, and testimony. They are based on the "Process of Making Chocolate Outline" in the Philadelphia Press' *Guide to Public Speaking*, 3rd edition. You will see the section of the presentation that is being narrated and then the sample slide.

Example:

"Hot chocolate. Chocolate bar. Chocolate fondue. Chocolate ice cream. Chocolate pudding. Chocolate mousse. And my all-time favorite...chocolate chip cookies fresh out of the oven with their ooey-gooey chocolate chips just melting in your mouth."

This slide serves as an example of chocolate items, including the favorite listed. They are simple, clear photos that you can view and still listen to the speaker without distraction.

Statistics:

"The bean comes from the cacao tree, which is found in over fifty tropical countries, according to the Equal Exchange Company, which specializes in chocolate, tea, and coffee ('Building a Vibrant Community')."

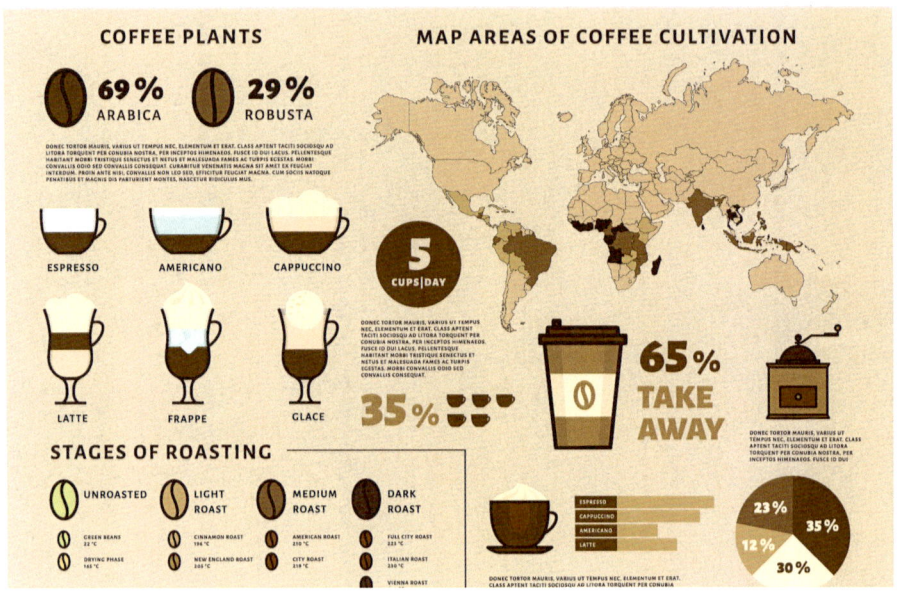

Testimony:

"Weis Market bakery manager, Courtney McCafferty, shares her insight on chocolate: "Chocolate is very sensitive. You have to melt it a certain way, to a certain temperature, so that when it is hardened, it's shiny and has a snap to it. The temperature or humidity in the room can affect it as well. It can also burn very easily."

In this case, the testimony is far too long to be put onto a slide. However, what is being described can be illustrated visually.

One last item to look at concerning content for your presentation is data visualization. David McCandless, a creative director, spoke at TEDGlobal shared this idea with his audience. "It feels like we're all suffering from information overload or data glut. And the good news is there might be an easy solution to that, and that's using our eyes more. So, visualizing information to see the patterns and connections that matter and then design that information makes more sense. It tells a story or allows us to focus only on the important information. Failing that, visualized information can look cool." His talk then went on to share ways to do just that. You can watch his talk here for more tips and tricks:

Now that you have written your presentation, it's finally time to plan your visual aid. To approach this section, we will discuss Dos and Don'ts.

Visual Aid Dos and Don'ts

1. Do keep your slides simple. A white or black background, not too much detail. Simple is easier to look at and digest. Consider personalizing the slides for your audience in the borders.

2. Do present a title slide and an outline at the beginning of your talk as two separate slides. Your title slide should have the title of your presentation along with your name. The outline slide should have a brief, bulleted overview of what is to follow. Think back to the thesis statement example on baseball earlier in the chapter (example below). These two elements are a very important part of your visual; however, do not let them compromise your introduction.

    a) You have several ways to grab your audience's attention and draw them in to want to listen to your presentation. They usually involve getting the audience curious about something. For instance, if you wanted to open your presentation with this question: What do the famous cellist, Yo-Yo Ma, CNBC's *Mad Money* host Jim Cramer, and retired basketball player Allison Feaster Strong have in common? The answer is they all graduated from Harvard University. If you have a title slide saying Harvard University, you will 'give away' the answer to the question. In this case, begin your presentation with a blank slide, so you do not compromise your creative introduction.

3. Do define any abbreviations used within your presentation. Once you have defined them, use them on your slides. Avoid using too many abbreviations on one slide. For example, if you explain how to use a scorecard at a baseball game, this entails using many abbreviations. The example below has several abbreviations listed and proves to be confusing and distracting as opposed to helpful.
4. Do use minimal short phrases, no paragraphs when using text on your slides. Your slide is not a classroom lecture with notes projected on the screen. It's an AID to your presentation.
5. Remember that anything you put on the screen is competition for your attention.
6. Do keep your audience in mind during your presentation. As you craft your talk and your visual aid, think about whether the audience will respond positively. Are you breaking down technical concepts and using analogies to help with their comprehension? Are there too many graphs on one slide? Have you prepared too much content for your allotted time? Your overall purpose is to convey a clear and concise message (thesis statement) to your audience. Do you accomplish this in the presentation?

Visual Aid Dos and Don'ts

Do keep your slides simple: a white or black backround

Don't have too much content or too many slides for your allotted time.

Now that we've looked at the Dos, let's discuss the Don'ts.

1. Don't start preparing for your presentation by putting your slides together first. Slides are visual aids and should be done **last**. Once you have written your presentation, then you can begin your slide preparation. As mentioned earlier, you can create a reference list during the research process for images, graphs, and media clips to include. Now is the time to retrieve the list and start creating.

2. Don't have too much content or too many slides for your allotted time. All of us have our own process when preparing a presentation. One part of the process that is key is practice. The chances are excellent that your talk needs to fit into a time frame.

   As you work on your presentation, take time to practice (without a visual aid). For example, use the baseball thesis referenced earlier. The three components of the presentation are changes to baseball, altering the rules of strategy, and umpire review announcements. After you have written your introduction and the first section on the changes to baseball, pause, and take time to practice. If you look at this from a 100-percentage point scale, your introduction and conclusion will each be 5 percent, and the body will be 90 percent.

   The three main points covered will each account for 30 percent. If you are allotted twenty minutes for a presentation, you may want to aim for a fifteen-minute presentation and a five-minute question and answer session. It is a delicate balance of planning. There are also instances where you allow for a Q & A, but there are no questions. In this case, your presentation will end early. Be prepared for that possibility.

   There should be a balance throughout your presentation. Try not to spend too much time in any one area. If you do, perhaps you need to revisit your thesis statement. Regardless, your content is what fills your time. The slides should reflect your content and match up with the timing of your talk. Whether you add or subtract slides as you work on your visual aid, you still have content that should last only the time that you are allowed. You will often present with co-workers or fellow students and have to split time between the group. In addition, the attendees have other commitments, and it's important to honor the time agreed upon.

3. Don't use the following on your slides: full sentences, paragraphs, several abbreviations, all capital letters, or several visuals on one slide. Your slides should have short key terms, phrases, and visuals to complement your content.

4. Don't put more than three or four key points on one slide. For business presentations, you should keep them as simple as possible.

5. Don't use a blue background for your slides, if possible. The knowledge website www.reference.com tells us that blue color is the hardest color for your eyes to process. If the background is blue, you are making it difficult for the viewer to focus, which isn't to say not to use blue at all on a slide, just don't use it as the background where most of the content is placed.

6. Don't rush through your presentation. Practice makes perfect. Practice as you create your talk and practice once you've completed the talk and with using visual aids. Doing so will help tremendously. In addition, be sure to practice WITH your speaking notes. Time yourself as you are practicing. Also, if you stumble as you practice, don't start over. Plenty of times when presenting you may falter a bit with your words, pronunciation, or just about anything. You will not say to an audience, "Oh, can I start over? I completely messed up that part there." No, you will have to just continue in spite of any missteps. If one of the famous Rockette dancers misses a step during the world-famous Radio City Christmas Spectacular, she will not ask to stop the show and start over. The show must go on and so must your presentation. The more you practice, the less likely a misstep is to happen.

7. Don't finish your presentation showing a media clip. Finish your presentation with your planned conclusion. You want the audience to remember you more than they remember the clip. Depending on the situation, you may need to end with works cited or a reference slide. If this is the case, work that into your conclusion. Remember that conclusions aren't afterthoughts or just a few sentences. They are the opportunity to review what you've discussed and wrap up your presentation in a thoughtful and perhaps creative or clever way. And always end with a "Thank You!"

Your conclusion may look like this:

So today, we have learned about the changes being implemented in Major League Baseball beginning in 2021. We've looked at changes to the baseball itself and the bases. We've discussed the rules that will affect coaching strategies and also the umpire review announcements that will most likely begin during postseason play in 2021.
Baseball is looked at as boring by many, even though it has been dubbed America's pastime

Several articles have additional information, and they are listed here on this slide. I'm also happy to forward that list to you.

The changes being executed this season won't take it to the level of excitement in hockey or soccer, but it is a start. As FOX'S MLB analyst and baseball player, Ben Verlander, says in his "The Good and Bad of Baseball's New Rules for the 2021 Season" web article,

"These rules will certainly change the way the game is played, but that isn't a bad thing. This game is always evolving, with players getting bigger and stronger and faster."

(SPEAKER NOTE – PAUSE HERE FOR EFFECT)
Thank you for listening. Any questions?

Using Visual Aids in the Business World

In a virtual presentation, slides are almost always used. They help the audience follow along with your presentation. The slides supplement what you say; they do not replace you. The slides should not be able to stand alone. They are for your audience to increase their understanding. They should also be simple and sophisticated.

When making a presentation for an organization, you should personalize your slides for your audience and your organization. Most companies will require you to use company branding, colors, and logos that are pre-approved and used by everyone in the organization. You can enhance the slides by using your audience's information. For example, if the slides are being presented to a specific department in an organization, you can include the department name on each slide, which helps create a connection. Images such as logos and photos also help to make connections. Make sure that you are using the images legally. Just because an image is on the internet does not mean it is up for grabs to use. (Note: classroom usage of images has a different set of guidelines under the Fair Use law) Be sure to gain permission to use images and credit the images on your slide as well. You can insert a small textbox next to the image and either name the source or the person who created the image.

You should also use the same "tone" within the presentation based on the audience. Use consistent and appropriate language for your audience. Look to your outline when getting ready to create your slides. The slides and their tone should be personalized for the audience.

Considerations of Visual Design

While you are designing the slides for your audience, be sure everything included is allowed. If you need any graphics or images from the audience's organization, reach out to the human resources or publications department. They can provide you with the appropriate items. As mentioned earlier, just because it exists on the web doesn't mean it's there for you to use for your purposes. In addition, presentations will often be re-used for more than one client, which is common practice and makes sense not to re-create a presentation every time you meet with a client. However, you must double and triple-check that any mention of the client's name is correct. The same with data. Re-using presentations can be helpful, but they can also compromise your credibility. Your client may think you put no work into the presentation because you missed changing the name on one slide. Mistakes can happen to anyone, but if you create a set of notes to reference, "always check slide 5" or "print presentation and highlight every mention of proper names (to catch a mistake in the client's name)," you lessen that possibility.

Text and fonts are very important. If the company's website uses a specific text or font, you can use the same or similar. Your font should be clear and professional as well. The images you use should be used with permission, but they should be clear and easy to see. Avoid distracting design elements such as too many patterns or objects/text flying in. Limit the number of words that appear on your slides. Keep type large enough for everyone to read. If presenting virtually, this is not as much of an issue as they are usually viewing on their computer screen and the present mode used usually fills up your screen. If presenting in person, take time as you prepare your talk to put the slide show on present mode and walk away from your computer screen. Can you see what is on the screen? While it's not an exact simulation of what will happen in person, it can give you an idea.

When you do present in person, take five minutes at the beginning or end of your presentation, and walk to the back of the room while your slides are up on the screen. Can you read them easily? Or you could ask someone who you know in the audience to take notes on the readability and visual effect as an audience member. Use that information moving forward. Note the font size and write it on a piece of paper and hang it nearby your computer. When you prepare your next presentation, use the information that you have saved to guide you.

Experts recommended using less than forty words per slide, a great target. However, your use will depend on the situation. If you need more than forty words on a slide, break your material up into two or three slides. The content will remain the same, so you aren't adding to your talk; you simply break the information into smaller chunks. Instances of not following this rule of forty words or less are prevalent in various industries. Follow along with necessary industry guidelines; however, when possible, follow our suggestions here. Always ask yourself if the information can be broken down.

One of the reasons to keep the text to a minimum on a slide is the idea mentioned above—that you are the star of the show, and your audience should be listening to you. When you have a slide filled with eight lines and three images, and you need to review each one—you'll be on line two, but the audience has already wandered down to the three bottom images and is not paying attention to you. By breaking this up, you are commanding their attention naturally. You have not given them too many distractions.

A popular response to defending more text on a slide is because the client will have the presentation and reference it for information post-presentation. Consider how you want to approach this. You want to have all information available but not too much on one slide. Break down what you can. There will always be exceptions, but try to do everything you can to have your presentation simply aid your talk. Use the option of additional handouts to supplement your presentation.

As mentioned earlier, your presentation will be filled with content. There are two types of content: quantitative and qualitative.

Quantitative content includes numbers, tables, diagrams, and charts. Qualitative content covers images, graphics, illustrations, and colors. You should have a balance of both and not overdo either. For example, using a white background with company color accents is a good balance of the graphics and illustrations. This way, the content you are conveying is easy to see and not hindered.

Use accepted symbols and abbreviations. We mentioned in the Do's and Don'ts, the first time you use a symbol or acronym or abbreviation, you should explain it. For example, if you are discussing data from the CDC, explain what the CDC is. You may think it's a common abbreviation. It is a well-known acronym, but you shouldn't assume we all know what it means. Let's look at the following sentence: The Centers for Disease Control and Prevention (CDC) feature notices of current infectious disease outbreaks and travel restriction notices on their website, which is what you would say within your talk. The slide itself may look like this:

Once you have established the abbreviation, you can continue to use it without spelling it out. Have the spelled-out words and abbreviation within your visual aid because your audience will see the words and abbreviation together to make them aware that you will be using it moving forward.

Four Golden Rules of Presentations

Aside from the Dos and Don'ts, we also abide by the Four Golden Rules in presentations. These Four Golden Rules are as follows:

1. Only use what is needed on each slide to aid the audience in understanding. Your message should not distract the audience.

2. Keep the slides as simple as possible. Don't lose your audience in a sea of graphs and overuse of text.

3. Have someone else proofread your visual aid. There is no room for errors. As mentioned earlier, if you are using a presentation that you have used before but with a different audience, be sure that you have updated all of the personalized information. Your audience WILL notice when there is a different company name or logo on a slide. That will convey carelessness to your audience and could damage your credibility.

4. Always have a backup plan for when something goes wrong—because it will. Anticipate issues and come up with alternative solutions. For example, if you are on a virtual call and the platform you are using isn't allowing you to share your screen, what do you do? What is your backup plan? In addition, have access to your presentation in as many ways as possible. Suggestions include:

- Email it to yourself and check that the file is properly working before you leave your home computer. You could even send it to two email addresses, your work and your home email.
- If you are presenting with a co-worker, email it to them also. If you are stuck in traffic or a plane with weather delays, your co-worker can go ahead and get started. Explaining to an audience or a client that you cannot begin because your co-presenter is the only person with the file will not sit well.
- Save it on a shared drive or Google drive.
- Put the file on a flash drive, and remember to bring the drive with you.
- Always check on the file as well. There is sometimes incompatibility between types of computers. Check the file name. Occasionally, a file gets saved differently and is inaccessible when you attempt to open it on a different computer. Doublecheck the files after they have been saved or arrive in your email's inbox.

Also, have your notes for your talk printed and ready to go. If technology fails, you can still present your ideas. You should have a backup plan if there is no access to your prepared visual aid. Imagine arriving to give a very important presentation on your laptop, and it begins to update as soon as you power the computer on. If you have your notes, you can begin without delay. Or you can use someone else's computer and use the USB drive to access your presentation. The time you take to plan for these types of situations could save you from being embarrassed and save your credibility.

Wrapping it all up

The more you practice, the better your presentation will be. Use your presentation notes and practice WITH your visual aids. Practicing your notes with your visual aids is far different than practicing with just your content. If you practice without the aid, it is very obvious to your audience. Be sure to write on your notecards when to change slides. Sometimes, even when you practice enough, the speaker sometimes gets distracted and forgets to advance the slides—especially when showing some type of media where the presenter needs to exit the slide and show a clip from the internet. Once they jump back into the presentation slides, they often forget where they were. Marking your notes will help to avoid this. You can write "click" or "advance" in the next section of your notes.

Relax! Try your best to relax as you present. If you have prepared and practiced to the best of your ability, you will be in good shape. In the words of inventor/scientist Alexander Graham Bell, "Before anything else, preparation is the key to success."

References:

Claire, A. (2016, December 21). *10 TED talks that used visual graphics to win the audience*. Inc.com. Retrieved August 3, 2022, from https://www.inc.com/anna-guerrero/10-ted-talks-that-used-visual-graphics-to-win-the-audience.html

Dobrin, S. et al. Technical Communication in the Twenty-First Century, 2nd Edition. 2009. Pearson.

FOX Sports. (2021, July 20). *The good and bad of baseball's new rules for the 2021 season*. FOX Sports. Retrieved August 3, 2022, from https://www.foxsports.com/stories/mlb/new-rules-minor-league-baseball-2021-season-ben-verlander

McCandless, D. (n.d.). *The beauty of Data Visualization*. David McCandless: The beauty of data visualization | TED Talk. Retrieved August 3, 2022, from https://www.ted.com/talks/david_mccandless_the_beauty_of_data_visualization

11

Virtual Meetings

Thomas Wright, PhD, Temple University
Maxine Gesualdi, PhD, West Chester University

As many organizations increase their reach around the world, meetings held through media technology have become commonplace. Virtual meetings, also referred to as videoconferences or web conferences, provide an opportunity to meet across physical distance through various technology platforms. Many best practices of face-to-face meetings apply to virtual meetings. However, virtual meetings introduce new variables and considerations for planners to ensure a successful session. This chapter will review the types of virtual meetings, the technology used to host them, and best practices for planning and conducting a virtual meeting.

Four Types of Virtual Meetings

Virtual meetings provide an opportunity for a geographically dispersed audience to convene in real-time. Therefore, a virtual meeting can replace any face-to-face meeting through the use of mediated technology. In addition, many virtual meeting technologies allow for recording, so the content of the meetings can be posted online or sent to people to watch after the initial event. In this way, virtual meetings can be a valuable communication tool.

Although ordinary, day-to-day meetings can be conducted virtually with minimal preparation, other types of virtual meetings require special attention. These are general webinars, training sessions, and team meetings.

General Webinars

A webinar is a meeting during which one person or a small group of people present to a large group of people. During a webinar, the speakers are the only people who can speak via voice technology, while the audience uses a typed messaging format to ask questions. Webinars provide a controlled environment for presenters to convey a message or teach about a topic. Examples of webinars are school board meetings or town halls with organizational leadership.

Training

Virtual training meetings have the same objective as in-person training: to help participants gain new knowledge or skills. However, virtual training meetings operate as a classroom and usually have a leader who is teaching to a small group. During these sessions, the leader often uses technology to interact with the participants. Technology is also used in virtual training to conduct learning checks and gather feedback from participants about the effectiveness of the training. Virtual training meetings can be brief, such as an hour or two, or much longer, such as a day-long or multi-day session.

Team Meetings

Teams are small groups of people within an organization focused on achieving a specific goal or completing a project. Teams are formed for short-term and long-term purposes. Conducting a team meeting virtually allows team members from all over the world to see each other in real-time. Virtual team meetings are often collaborative, with all team members contributing to the conversation to help keep the project moving forward and meet the team and organizational goals.

Planning a Virtual Meeting

Putting together a virtual meeting follows many of the same steps as face-to-face meetings. These common steps include setting a date and time, inviting participants, and creating an agenda. Because virtual meetings add the variable of mediated spaces for the meeting, several added considerations are needed to plan a virtual meeting, including selecting the technology, assigning roles for meeting participants, and practicing with the technology.

Selecting Technology

The available media technology for virtual meetings is rapidly evolving. Because many organizations pivoted to all-online operations during the COVID-19 pandemic, tech companies rushed to fill the need for virtual meeting platforms. As a result, it is impossible to review all tech available because it is ever-evolving. However, there are two significant categories of meeting platforms: web browser and server-based.

Categories of Virtual Meeting Platforms

One major category of virtual meeting technology platforms is the **web browser meeting platform**. This type of technology operates using standard web browsers such as Google Chrome. Users have to open a web browser, open a link to the meeting, and join the meeting in progress. Users may need to download specific software for the meeting platform, but usually, these are small programs and easy to run. Anyone with an internet connection, a device such as a laptop or mobile phone, and a web browser can join these web-based meetings. In addition, participants can share their computer screens with others in the meetings. Web meeting platforms are usually optimized for desktop or laptop computer use. However, mobile devices can also be used, sometimes with less functionality than the computer interface. Examples of these platforms are Zoom, GoToMeeting, VIA3, and Wonder.

Another major category of virtual meeting technology platforms is the **server-based platform**. This type of platform uses proprietary technology to host meetings. Users often need to pay for and download a program to a computer to participate in the meetings. Some organizations buy licenses for these programs so that all members can download the programs. A centralized web server hosts the meeting and stores the presentation materials. Some server-based platforms also provide an optional meeting professional to help set up and facilitate the meeting. Examples of server-based platforms are Webex and Microsoft Live Meeting.

Platform Features

Although the web platforms differ, based on how they are hosted, they share many of the same features for audio, video, document sharing, application and desktop sharing, whiteboards, chat, polling, and recording.

Audio. Good quality audio is of utmost importance in a virtual meeting. Most virtual meeting platforms allow you to use a headset for better microphone and speaker quality. In addition, there is a mute feature that allows all participants only to be heard when speaking. In addition, many platforms allow you to adjust your audio to eliminate background noise and increase your voice amplification. The audio in a virtual meeting is usually two-way unless the meeting organizer turns off this feature to limit audio to the designated speakers, such as in a webinar.

Video. What makes virtual meetings unique is the ability to see other people even though you are not in the same room or even in the same country! Video for virtual meetings requires a good, high-speed internet connection and a webcam. Video sharing is also possible, with short video clips working best through the platforms. Most platforms have an option to keep the web camera on or off. Keeping the web camera on as much as possible increases engagement with the other meeting attendees.

Document Sharing. Within virtual meeting technology platforms, meeting leaders and participants can share their computer screens or share a document from a centralized repository in a server-based platform. This feature allows for collaboration among meeting attendees. The documents shared can be from word processing programs such as Microsoft Word, presentations such as Google slides, pdf files, and other web browser tabs. In addition, document sharing allows for animations in presentations and real-time collaboration on shared documents such as Google Docs.

Application and Desktop Sharing. Beyond individual documents and web browser tabs, virtual meeting technology platforms also allow you to share individual applications through screen sharing, which is particularly useful during team meetings when participants may need to collaborate on specialized software programs to complete a task or project.

Whiteboards. Some virtual meeting platforms feature a whiteboard or a virtual tool to draw and write through the computer screen. Virtual meeting whiteboards function like a whiteboard and markers in a face-to-face meeting venue. Whiteboards can be enabled or disabled in many virtual meeting platforms and allow users to collaborate through drawing, list-making, and brainstorming exercises. Whiteboards are particularly useful in team meetings.

Chat. Virtual meeting platforms also include a text-based messaging function usually labeled as chat. This feature allows the meeting leaders to type messages to participants publicly or privately. Chat also allows individual meeting participants to message each other. The chat function is tailored to the meeting purpose by allowing meeting leaders to restrict the messages to be sent, such as only allowing messages to display to all participants. The chat transcription is saved on many meeting platforms. In some larger meetings, a designated person should monitor the chat for questions and issues, which allows the meeting presenters to focus on their content and not be distracted or interrupted by the chat. Chat is particularly helpful for sharing links to meeting resources and providing feedback to the meeting leaders.

Polling. Some meeting platforms allow for real-time polling of the audience. Meeting leaders can set up polling questions in advance of the meeting, and participants can select answers to the poll questions at any time during the meeting. Leaders can then share and discuss the results from the polls. Some platforms also allow leaders to add poll questions in real-time during the meeting. Poll questions help increase engagement with large audiences. They also provide meeting hosts with a way to check in with an audience, especially large audiences that are not easily seen via the video feature of the virtual meeting.

Recording. Many virtual meeting platforms allow you to record your meetings as they occur and post them later. Some platforms have cloud-based storage for these recordings and basic editing capabilities for the videos. You are also often able to download the meeting recordings from the platform's cloud. Meeting hosts can decide how they will share the videos for those who may want to revisit the meeting content or those who could not attend. Let the meeting participants know ahead of time that the meeting is being recorded. Many platforms will allow you to record, pause, and restart the recording automatically. Many platforms also include a pre-recorded message for anyone who logs on to know that the meeting is being recorded. These recordings help create a permanent record of the meeting event and provide ways to communicate your messages from the meeting after the session ends.

Make Your Outline

Effective meetings include a solid plan. There is a joke in popular discourse that pokes fun at meetings that could have been an email. Good meeting planning avoids this situation and ensures that all participants find value in your meeting.

First, a meeting should have goals and objectives. **Goals** are the big picture of why the meeting is essential. The meeting's goals should be aligned with the goals of the organization or project. **Objectives** are the actionable and concrete outcomes from the meeting. Ask yourself questions about why you call a meeting and what you plan to accomplish during the session. Answering these questions can help you set goals and objectives. If it is difficult to establish these goals and objectives, perhaps you should reconsider the need for the meeting or think of other ways to accomplish your goals. In addition to the goals and objectives, any presentation during a meeting that lasts for more than a few minutes should have an outline. The first type of outline you should create is a meeting **agenda**. The agenda is an outline of all the topics to be covered during the meeting and a speaker for each topic. If a meeting requires group input or discussion or voting, then the agenda should indicate where that input or discussion or voting will occur during the meeting.

The agenda will keep the meeting on track and allow you to achieve your goals and objectives. The meeting content on the agenda must help you meet your goals and objectives. It would be best if you also considered the time it would take to cover all the agenda items and ensure you can cover it all in the time you've allotted for the meeting.

Assign Roles and Responsibilities

A successful meeting includes people who know why they are there and what role they play. Therefore, the meeting organizer should assign roles to participants based on what actions they should take during the meeting. Here are some typical meeting roles:

Project Lead

A project lead, also known as a *meeting host*, is responsible for ensuring the meeting content is planned and delivered. Sometimes the project lead is also the meeting organizer. However, sometimes the meeting organizer plays more of a behind-the-scenes role and assigns someone to lead the meeting as the project lead.

The project lead acts as the meeting host and manages the meeting agenda outline. This person makes sure all tasks on the agenda are completed. They may also design and present all the content of the meeting. The project lead will also arrange for any follow-up needed after the meeting and make sure meeting records are kept, such as recording the virtual meeting and meeting minutes.

Presenters

The meeting organizer or the project lead should make sure presenters are ready for the meeting. Next, presenters deliver the meeting content. In this role, presenters should have their content outline or prepared presentation. No presenters should ever wing it. Instead, the presenters should practice their material enough times to deliver extemporaneously and professionally during the meeting. Presenters should also be given the meeting goals, objectives, and agenda to know how their part fits into the overall meeting.

Designing and Creating Presentations

In a virtual meeting, presentations must translate over the technology platform so that the audience can understand the content. Therefore, presenters need to consider how their presentation will look and sound to the virtual audience. Many programs like Microsoft PowerPoint and Google Slides work efficiently with web- and server-based platforms. Other tools like polling software and videos should be practiced to ensure compatibility. Because technology can sometimes be fickle, all presenters should have a Plan B, a low-tech version of their content, if the presentation can't be shown or the video does not work.

If the meeting has more than one presenter, the meeting organizer or project lead should coordinate the presenters' content. It is helpful to gather any prepared content a day or two ahead of the meeting so that the organizer or project lead can ensure that the content matches the expectations set out in the goals, objectives, and agenda for the meeting. If any of the content is not aligned, the organizer or project lead can work with individual presenters to tweak the material to fit the meeting better.

Invite Audience

The meeting organizer or project lead should ensure that the audience is notified of the meeting as soon as the date and time are set. Online calendar tools or meeting organization tools such as Calendly can invite large groups to a meeting. It is best to inform the audience members of any meeting prep work they need to do, such as reviewing documents or gathering ideas on the topics from the meeting agenda. You may sometimes need to find out information from your audience ahead of the meeting, such as their current thoughts on the meeting topic. You can do this through formal and informal electronic surveys. After the meeting, you should make sure that the audience understands their role in meeting follow-up tasks.

Rehearse

A good meeting runs smoothly, which takes preparation. When you add technology in a virtual meeting, that preparation needs some special attention. First, you should always test your technology to ensure it is working as you expect, including your meeting platform and any technology for delivering meeting content. Then, ideally, you should schedule a run-through with the presenters or as a separate session before the meeting when you run through the entire content. Or, it can be done briefly before the meeting time by asking presenters to join the meeting fifteen to thirty minutes ahead of time to practice switching between presenters and their content. To see and hear what the audience will hear, you can record the rehearsal and play it back.

In addition to running through the content, you should practice the meeting platform features such as chat and whiteboard. Then, have the people in the practice session use these tools in various ways to ensure that they work as you expect.

Virtual meeting platforms also come with specific pitfalls that you should anticipate. First, it would help if you prepared for any of the technology to stop working altogether. It would be best to plan how to handle someone who is not invited to the meeting who somehow joins in and takes over with inappropriate video or audio feed. Finally, it would help if you planned to assist an audience member or presenter with technical issues. If you think through these common problems, you will be able to ensure a successful meeting.

Conduct the Meeting: Day of Event

On the day of the meeting, you need to make sure the final touches are ready for the event. First, ensure your physical location is prepped and ready, which includes making sure the background of your camera angle looks professional and tidy or that you have a professional virtual background set, if available on your meeting platform.

Even if you have conducted a run-through, you should still log on early, at least fifteen minutes before start time, to test the technology one more time, which will give you added confidence in running a smooth meeting. You can ask all presenters to join you, or you can do this on your own.

Greet attendees as they log in to the meeting session, which allows for a relaxed beginning and provides you with a way to connect with individual audience members. The connection will help increase participation throughout the meeting.

One of the most respectful things you can do is make sure you start the meeting on time, which shows that you understand the value of your presenters' and audience members' time. It will also ensure that you have enough time to cover the items on your agenda. If the meeting is one where only a few people present while everyone else listens, try to engage the non-presenters every ten minutes or so. For example, you can use the chat feature, polling software, platform-reaction buttons, or ask people to chime in through their audio, which keeps your audience focused on the meeting content and gets them through to the end of the agenda without them disengaging from your meeting content.

At the end of the meeting, announce the end of the agenda items. At this point, you can ask for any last thoughts from the audience or presenters if there is time. Also, you should make sure that everyone understands the next steps and what is expected of all people in attendance. Lastly, thank everyone for attending, which helps put a definitive ending to the session and leaves participants with a positive feeling about the meeting and whatever comes next.

Follow-Up

The first step in following up after a meeting is a formal debrief. A debrief is a session with presenters that discusses how they thought the meeting went and what needs to be considered for future meetings. While it is still fresh in your mind, note what worked well and what may need to be done differently next time. Next, send a follow-up communication to all participants, including a note of thanks, action items that need to be completed, reminders of due dates, announcements of the next meeting date and time, links to a recording of the session, any feedback from the presenters on the meeting session, and instructions for participants on how to offer any additional input from the meeting. Finally, make sure you provide clear instructions on how the participants should execute their follow-up tasks and how you will be following up to ensure completion.

Overall, a virtual meeting follows the same best practices as face-to-face meetings. The difference is the variable of technology and bridging space through mediated platforms. Taking time to carefully set up the technology, outlining a solid agenda, assigning roles, creating engaging content, rehearsing, and following up after the meeting will set you up for success.

Etiquette Tips for Participants

As a meeting participant who is not a presenter, you have a unique responsibility to help the meeting run smoothly. Here are some tips to consider:

- Be aware of your background: Make sure the background of your camera angle is not distracting to other participants. Some meeting platforms allow you to use a virtual background to hide your room if that will be more appropriate.

- Wear appropriate attire: Dress to the expectations of the organization holding the meeting. Even though the meeting is virtual, it's a good idea to think about the virtual meeting the same way as you'd think about being in the same room as the other participants. So, therefore, you should dress for the occasion similar to the in-person meeting.

- Handle distractions before the virtual meeting starts: When we have meetings on virtual platforms, we can sometimes be interrupted by other people in our household, pets, or outside noises. We can even be distracted by other things on our computers like social media or other alerts. Disable any sounds for incoming emails. Alert others in your location about the meeting time so that they can avoid the area. Turn off other devices.

- Use voice appropriately when participating: It is easy to adjust our microphones and speakers through meeting platforms. Make sure your settings are correct via the audio testing features available in virtual meeting platforms. Ensure that you are speaking up and articulating so that all can hear. Through a virtual platform, it is sometimes helpful to be a little more animated than when we are in person so that your energy can translate across the technology.

- Do not eat during the virtual meeting: Because the camera is focused on us at all times, eating during a virtual meeting, unless explicitly allowed, should be avoided and can be a major distraction for the participants. If you must eat something, it is best to temporarily turn off your camera while eating and turn it back on when finished.
- Make eye contact when possible: Because virtual meetings are meant to simulate face-to-face interaction, making eye contact with the camera helps the other participants feel like you're engaging directly with them. It also helps you seem engaged throughout the meeting, even if you're not talking.
- Do not perform other tasks while in the virtual meeting: Respect the presenters by not multitasking during the meeting. Instead, put away other work and devices so that you can be fully engaged in the meeting content.
- Remember the mute button: Always mute your microphone when you are not speaking. You want to respect the presenters by not inadvertently interrupting them with sound from your location. You also want to avoid any potential embarrassment of making any comments or noises you think are only heard by you but can be heard by all participants.
- Practice patience: Virtual meetings can sometimes be hard to engage with initially, especially if people have technical difficulties or are hard to follow. Being patient with the presenters will help you get more out of the meeting and focus on the message instead of any tech mishaps.

Moderating Virtual Panels and Presentations

Thomas Wright, PhD, Temple University
Maxine Gesualdi, PhD, West Chester University

When you think of group presentations, you often think of class projects or group meetings. In these types of group presentations, individual speakers often present small segments in an overall cohesive meeting. These types of presentations can be classified as oral reports. You may not be as familiar with other types of group presentations such as colloquiums, symposiums, and forums. According to Floyd and Cardon (2020), colloquiums are group presentations during which group members discuss a topic among themselves in front of an audience in a conversational style. Symposiums are group presentations during which members of a small group make formal, individual presentations on the same topic. Forums are group presentations similar to colloquiums but include some interaction between the audience and the speakers. Symposiums, colloquiums, and forums are conducted in a panel format. A panel is the name for the group of people participating in the group meeting.

Panel presentations have specific requirements for success. Unlike oral reports, a panel presentation is usually made up of people who have interacted very little before the meeting, which can pose some challenges. In addition, a panel has a leader, or moderator, who must plan and orchestrate the presentation. The moderator has to work diligently to ensure a successful panel. In this chapter, you will learn about the role of the panel moderator, best practices for planning, organizing, and moderating a panel, methods for guiding a question-and-answer session during a panel, and best practices for panel moderators and participants.

Moderating a Panel

Panel presentations have many moving parts that can make them difficult to manage. What can go wrong? The panelists may not be prepared or know what to expect. The moderator may not be equipped to lead the discussion, or the audience members may hijack the meeting during the question-and-answer portion. One panelist may dominate the discussion.

One way to avoid all these issues is to have a well-prepared moderator. A **moderator** often designs the panel, plans the presentation, leads the discussion, manages a question-and-answer period, and follows up, as needed, after the panel. Thus, moderating takes as much preparation time as giving the entire presentation yourself. The following sections provide details on the main tasks of the moderator that help ensure a positive experience for everyone.

Decide on a Topic

Sometimes the moderator is brought into the planning process after the panel's topic is selected. However, sometimes moderators are planning a panel from the first step, which is topic selection. This can happen when a special event is being planned, like a conference or a workshop. A moderator may be part of the special event planning and may be asked to develop a panel from start to finish.

When deciding on a topic, you should review the event's overall purpose and the panel portion. Ask yourself how the topic can align with the purpose and augment the event by adding to the program's content. Next, brainstorm some topics that will complement the overall program. Think about the types of panelists who could add expertise to the panel's topic. Once you narrow down the list to the topic you think will be best, you may need to get approval from the event organizer.

When developing the topic for the panel, make sure you develop two or three main points you want your audience to take away from the panel. To do this, you should also analyze your audience.

Analyze the Audience

Panels are part of a larger event that has a specific audience in place. For example, panels at professional association meetings are members of that professional organization. Panels designed for workplace workshops are made up of the members of that workplace or specific types of employees such as managers or supervisors. Sometimes the panel presentation will be part of the program that everyone attends. Sometimes audience members or attendees can choose to attend your panel from a list of concurrent panels.

For your panel, you should focus on your expected audience. Some questions you may ask are the following:

- What are the demographics of the audience?
- What time of the day is your panel?
- Will the audience be eating during the panel?
- Will the panel begin or end the day?
- What prior knowledge does your audience have on the topic?
- If the panel is on a controversial topic, will audience members be hostile toward the topic, agreeable, neutral, or have mixed attitudes?
- What technology platform will be used to host the virtual panel, and how will the audience interact through the technology?

Answers to these questions will help you develop a better panel presentation because you can tailor the session to your audience. As a result, a tailored presentation will be better received and more meaningful for your audience.

Select Speakers

Most likely, when you were deciding on your topic, you had some panelists in mind. However, to ensure a successful panel, you need to analyze the potential panelists and their contributions to the session.

You should choose speakers who have credibility on the topic and an important perspective--from people with first-hand experience or professional expertise on the topic. You should make sure you have diversity in your panel, including diversity in race, gender, age, and other demographic categories. It would be best to consider the diversity of worldviews, outlooks, and stances on your topic, which will ensure a lively discussion that does not suffer from groupthink and will illuminate many different voices. A panel should showcase a range of people and perspectives.

In addition, you should invite panelists who are dynamic presenters! You can have someone with a lot of expertise on the panel, but if they can't express themselves in the panel format, they will not help your panel be successful.

Lastly, you should recruit one or two extra panelists in case one of your panelists cancels. You can explain to these people that they are backup selections, and you will let them know if they are needed.

Provide Clear Expectations for the Panelists

Now that you have selected your panelists and they have accepted your invitation, you need to provide clear expectations for the panel presentation. The first step is to send every panelist an email or other written communication that leaves no doubt about their role. The communication is an agreement of sorts between you and the panelists. The communication should outline:

Your Vision for the Panel

Explain to the panelists what you are trying to accomplish through the panel, including how the panel fits into the event and what you hope the audience will take away from the session.

Explain What Aspects of the Topic Each Panelist Should Address

You should include what you hope each panelist will talk about during the panel. Be very specific here. For example, suppose your panel is about student success at the college, and one of your panelists is from the college's tutoring center. In that case, you should spell out that you want the panelist from the tutoring center to talk about what the tutoring center offers to ensure student success. Do not be afraid to be direct about what you hope each person will talk about during the panel, which will ensure that each panelist is speaking to their expertise and will avoid repetition by the panelists.

Explain the Logistics of the Event

Tell the panelists the time and date of the event. Include the name of the technology platform and instructions on how to access the technology. Explain the format of the panel and agenda (see the section below for how to develop an agenda and outline). Tell the panelists what time they have for prepared remarks, if visual aids are needed, and what types are appropriate, and what type of questions you expect from the audience. Let panelists know the information they may need in addition to you, such as the main event organizer or the other panelists. And let them know how to reach you if they have any questions before the event.

Give Panelists Days and Times for a Pre-Event Meeting

You should provide a few dates and times to choose from for a pre-event meeting. You can try to meet with all the panelists at one time or choose to have individual meetings. It is very important to have at least one meeting with the panelists prior to the event to reiterate the initial communication and discuss the event. You can also provide the final agenda for the meeting and the questions you will use to guide the panelists through the discussion.

Ask Panelists to Send You an Up-To-Date Resume or Bio

You can use this information to draft your introductory remarks and write up an overview for a presentation program leaflet or website. Bio information may also be needed if you are writing a program for the event.

Create an Agenda and Outline

Now that your panelists are on board and you've set expectations, it's time to create a detailed plan for the panel presentation. Start by creating a detailed agenda with times for each part of the presentation. Some considerations for the agenda are as follows:

Introduction

You should carefully plan what you will say in the introduction to the panel. You are setting the tone for the entire event. You need to make sure you nail the intro! Use the resumes or bio from the panelists to draft a brief introduction of each person. It would be best to prepare a short overview of the panel's topic of discussion and a list of ground rules for the panelists and audience members about what to expect during the session. You should deliver this information extemporaneously, engaging with the audience, using best practices of public speaking delivery and virtual meetings. Be sure you have the phonetic spelling of each panelist's name so you can make sure you're pronouncing the names correctly. At the end of the introduction, your audience should know why the panel has been convened, a general overview of the topic to be discussed, and what they should expect from the presentation.

Prepared Remarks or an Opening Question

You can decide to have the speakers each give a short, 3-5 minute overview of their expertise and their connection to the panel's topic. This approach has some pros and cons. Allowing each speaker time for opening remarks can positively orient the audience to the speakers and allow the speakers to settle into the session. However, it can sometimes lead to a formal tone that may not be what you are trying to accomplish. If you choose to start the panel without the prepared remarks, you should use an opening question that all panelists will have a chance to answer. This opening question should be thought-provoking and allow each panelist to discuss their expertise as part of the answer. In addition, the opening question should be general enough that each panelist would be able to contribute to the discussion in a meaningful way.

Outline of Questions for the Panelists on the Topic

To ensure your goals for the panel are met, draft a series of questions for the panelists that you will ask in succession. At times, the panelists will have a natural flow between topics that you can follow and ask follow-up questions. However, if the panelists do not flow naturally through a conversation, you should ask them questions to keep the conversation going throughout the meeting time. In addition, you should prepare more questions than you need in case the discussion goes by at a faster pace than you expect.

Question and Answer Period

If your panel is a forum-style group presentation, you will have a question and answer (Q&A) session. Make sure you allow ample time for this session. See the section in this chapter about how to organize the Q&A session.

Closing

After the final discussion question or after the Q&A, allow each panelist to give a closing thought. Carefully plan what you will say to summarize the session and give your audience

food for thought after leaving the panel. Some ideas for your closing include a roundup of the key points you want your audience to take away from the panel or asking a forward-thinking question about the topic. Finally, make sure that you thank the panelists and the audience.

Time To Mingle

Make sure you leave some time after the panel presentation for speakers to interact with each other and possibly audience members. This time is important for networking and allowing the panelists to have a pleasant experience. It will be uncomfortable for the panelists to be hurriedly cut off from the meeting session. Make sure you allow time for the end of the panel to be low stress. You can do this by making sure you have enough time at the end of your meeting to allow for mingling within the meeting platform with or without the audience present. Make sure your panelists know that they can stick around after the formal panel is over.

Plan the Question-and-Answer Portion

Although it seems simple, a question and answer (Q&A) portion of a panel presentation can go awry easily because the Q&A is part of the panel presentation that the moderator and panelists cannot control. Here are some critical considerations for moderating a successful Q&A period.

Plan How and When You Will Solicit Questions

You should have the amount of time allotted for Q&As stated in the agenda, and the program, which will ensure that the panelists and the audience are ready for the Q&A. Consider the logistics of the technology platform and how the questions will be asked. Will you solicit questions from audience members ahead of time via an email or survey? Will you be using an interactive tech platform where members can unmute themselves and ask questions, or will it be a webinar format where the questions must be asked in writing via a chat tool on the platform? Will you have an assistant who will monitor a chat feature on the technology platform?

Gathering written questions can make it easier to manage a Q & A session. Having written questions allows the moderator to select the most relevant or thought-provoking questions that will further the agenda of the panel presentation. Having written questions also allows for better control over the time of the Q&A because no one person can dominate the session. However, if written questions are not possible, the moderator can still manage the time during live questions. Just be aware that you may have to jump in to cut people off if the Q&A session starts to go off track. It is also easier to enlist another member of the event staff or a friend in the audience to monitor the chat simultaneously, and you perform other moderating duties during the panel. Most tech platforms allow you to designate a meeting co-host who will be able to monitor the chat.

Jot Down Your Questions as the Panelists are Presenting

Having your questions ready can alleviate any dead air if the audience does not ask questions at the start of the Q&A. Listen carefully throughout the panel presentation for areas that could use additional probing through questions. Have your questions ready throughout the Q&A session in case there is a lull.

Ask the Panelists if They Have Any Questions for the Other Panelists

You can gather questions panelists have for each other prior to the session or ask them any questions during the Q&A session. You can use the panelists' questions to start the Q&A or during the session if there is a lull from the audience. If you have these questions ahead of time, you can put them in an order that makes logical sense to keep the Q&A session flowing.

Manage Time Wisely

When there are about eight to ten minutes left in the panel presentation timeslot, announce that you will take one more question. After that question, move into the final remarks and the closing. Keeping close track of time ensures that the end of the panel time is not rushed.

Moderator Checklist

Setting up a panel can be overwhelming! But it is rewarding to bring together a panel of experts and diverse voices to help make an event more exciting and engaging. Here is a summary of the key considerations to be made by a panel moderator:

Before the Event
- Decide on topic
- Analyze audience
- Invite panelists, send them details, and meet with them
- Gather panelist information to assist with introductory remarks
- Prepare agenda and your remarks (introduction, closing)
- Work with event organizers on logistical needs such as the tech platform for the meeting, payments or honorariums for the panelists, writing segments for an event program, and so forth.
- Make sure you have contact information for a tech customer service person as a resource if you have any trouble during the panel.

The Day of the Event
- Arrive at the virtual room early to make sure the meeting platform is working.
- Have a last-minute check-in with the panelists prior to the audience arriving. Ensure the panelists are comfortable with the technology and understand the signals you will use to keep time during their remarks.
- Keep time for each portion of the panel presentation.
- Make sure the conversation flows and that all voices are heard. Don't be afraid to interrupt. For example, if one person is dominating, you can say, "I don't think we've heard from (name of other panelists)." Or "I'd like to move to another aspect of this topic." This statement will keep the conversation flowing.
- If the panel's topic is controversial, make sure you monitor the panel discussion to ensure that the conversation remains civil and respectful. Do not be afraid to respectfully call out panelists who are being rude or uncivil.

- Manage the Q&A time
- Ensure that enough time remains for a leisurely ending
- Thank the audience and the panelists

After the Event
- Send thank-you notes to the panelists
- Send any questions you receive after the event for the panelists to the panelists
- If you or the event managers collected any post-meeting feedback from the audience, evaluate the feedback and share anything relevant with the panelists. If no formal feedback was collected, be sure to share any informal feedback you've received.

What If You're a Panelist?

You may be involved in a group presentation as a panelist. Although less work than serving as the moderator, you still need to be prepared and polished. If you've been asked to be a panelist, you should incorporate the following best practices to engage with the audience.

Ensure you Know What's Expected

Good panel moderators will spell out what you should expect as a panelist. If your moderator or panel organizer has not discussed specifics with you, make sure you ask questions about the topic, use of opening remarks, audience profile, time allotted for the panel, Q&A time limits, and technology to be used. You should also understand the need for any visual aids and what formats to prepare them in, and if you have to submit them ahead of time. Make sure to have an up-to-date bio or resume to share with the moderator. Also, make sure you know about any pre-meeting times and what time you should arrive at the virtual meeting room. And, make sure you're prepared to deliver a professional and polished presentation using best practices of public speaking delivery.

Prepare Opening and Closing Remarks

Even if they aren't part of the official expectations, you should prepare some opening remarks introducing yourself and your expertise related to the panel topic. You should do the same for closing remarks. Closing remarks may change as the panel unfolds, but in general, you should prepare a summation of your thoughts on the topic and reiterate your position and expertise in the area.

Gather Important Contact Information

You should have contact information for the moderator and the organizer of the meeting, which includes mobile phone numbers in case of emergency on the day of the event and tech support contacts to help with any computer issues.

Connect With the Other Panelists

A panel is an opportunity for networking and growing your professional network. Make sure you know how to contact your fellow panelists, which can help you plan your remarks and any follow-up you want to do after the panel is over.

Do a Trial Run of the Technology

When technology is involved, whatever can go wrong usually does. So, make sure you do a trial run with whatever technology is being used for the meeting, including downloading any software, testing cameras and microphones, and logging into the room to make sure you can enter the virtual meeting on the day and time of the panel.

Be Prepared to Be Assertive

In a panel situation, there may be less emphasis on taking turns than in an oral report. Therefore, you need to be ready to jump in if you are being ignored or if someone is monopolizing the time. Good phrases to use to cut in are, "I'd like to expand on the previous point" or "I have something to add here that will add value to the discussion." In addition, you may need to be more assertive than you'd be in regular conversation during a panel.

Be Prepared for the Unexpected

Although you have prepared your remarks and understand the expectations, many things can derail a panel. Be prepared for technology failures, monopolizing panelists or audience members, inept moderators, and off-topic discussions. You should go into a panel with a mindset of adapting, as needed, to whatever situation arises. The best thing you can do is be prepared for what you want to say but expect the unexpected.

Thank the Moderator and the Meeting Organizer

Make sure you thank the moderator and meeting organizer on the day of the event. Another nice touch would be to send an email or mail a card to them after the event. Beyond professional courtesy, these notes can keep you at the top of their mind for future speaking opportunities.

Make Connections with Those Who Follow Up with You

Frequently, audience members or other panelists may want to connect with you to discuss future speaking opportunities, future projects, or even job opportunities. Make sure you ask the moderator and event organizer to pass along any follow-up they get related to your remarks so you can make connections. In addition, during any time left for mingling after the panel, make sure you take down contact information for potential professional connections.

Have Fun

Overall, a panel is a unique opportunity to showcase your expertise and connect with other people with similar interests in a topic. So put forth your best professional delivery skills and enjoy the spotlight.

References

Clark, D. (2018). How to Prepare for a Panel. *Harvard Business Review Digital Articles,* 2-4.

Floyd, K., & P. W. Cardon, (2020). B*usiness and professional communication.* McGraw-Hill Education.

Friedman, M. (1999). Guidelines for moderating a panel. *Public Relations Tactics, 6*(6), 14-15.

Kaeter, M. (1994). Perfect panel presentations. Training, 11. Retrieved from http://libproxy.temple.edu/login?url=https://www-proquest-com.libproxy.temple.edu/trade-journals/perfect-panel-presentations/docview/203401373/se-2?accountid=14270

Kerber, L. K. (2008). Conference Rules, 2: Everything you need to know about introducing speakers and running a panel discussion. *Perspectives on History, 46(6),* 39-40.

Koza, M. P. (2006). Keys to Leading Lively Panel Discussions. *Njbiz, 19*(1), 11.

Speaking on a Panel. (2006). *Broker Magazine, 8*(7), 6-13.

Whiteman, L. (2009). Showcase skills when moderating panels. *Federal Times, 45*(21), 18.

13

Online Interviewing in a Post-Pandemic World

Pam Marshall, Rowan University
J. Kanan Sawyer, PhD, West Chester University

For your parents' generation, interviewing was a straightforward process. They looked in the newspaper and found a good ad. They sent in the one and only résumé that they had. They got called in for an interview (especially if they knew someone at the company because nepotism was king!) and then they went to the company to talk to the boss. That's it. But that's not it anymore. Almost every aspect of interviewing has changed and if you don't change with it then you will likely find yourself in a job that does not fulfill you and with less pay or benefits than what you deserve.

First, why the change? You may already know the answer to this. The world changed and so interviews have changed along with it. Technology has widened the field. Now a person in Japan can find a job posted for a company in Topeka, Kansas. Now a person with a background in R Programming can find a position with a startup CRO (yes — both of those things are real) that does not yet have an established reputation. Technology has dramatically changed access to information, candidates, and companies.

Second, we had a global pandemic. In 2019 and through 2021 (or later depending on when this chapter is read), the COVID-19 pandemic forced most of the population indoors. We were physically separated from one another and yet, hiring did not stop. Beyond the essential workers that already had positions, some doctors and emergency workers heeded desperate calls from corona virus-stricken areas across the globe. The Gig Economy became more than some dude in his mom's basement writing gaming codes. Now, single moms, college students, and grandparents were all searching online for work that was either essential or remote. The need for IT professionals spiked as we went from in-person meetings to, in some cases, all corporate communication moving online. In June 2021, Business Insider reported that nearly 40% of those who had jobs would consider quitting even after pandemic contraction rates have receded if employers do not allow them to continue to work from home or remotely (Duffy, 2021).

In this new world, the IT explosion has meant that nearly all aspects of work that *had* to move online found a means of doing so and people became comfortable with the process. That comfort increases the likelihood that, even when a company can safely interview you in-person, they may opt to go through a fully or at least partially online interview process. Have you ever used Microsoft Teams? Do you know how to facilitate breakout rooms in Zoom? Are you comfortable using Google Hangouts for professional purposes? If you answered no to any of these questions or even took a minute to assess your comfort level on those platforms, then you would do well to read on. In today's world, you must be prepared to interview online.

Looking Ahead

The aim of this chapter is to help you view the online interview process as comfortable. While you may still be a bit nervous about the interview (and butterflies are completely normal), you can rest assured that after reading the material here, you will know the steps to take to make your interview successful. We will take you through the various types of interviews that may occur online, various mediums for interviewing, necessary preparations, how to keep organized in an online interview setting, and how to answer questions effectively as well as strategies for engaging with the interviewer through questions that you ask and follow-up efforts that you make.

Types of Interviews

Definitionally, **interviews** are two-way, relational communication exchanges, which serve as a specialized form of oral task-related communication. The task? That depends on the type of interview. Different situations call for different types of interviews (Auerbach, 2018; Berkelaar & Murphy, 2017). Those interview types include:

- **Informational** (applicant-initiated, typically pre-interview)
- **Performance** (employer-initiated, regular interval work assessment)
- **Counseling** (applicant or employer-initiated, therapeutic focus)
- **Interrogation** (employer-initiated, investigatory)
- **Grievance** (applicant-initiated, conflict resolution)
- **Exit** (employer-initiated, offer employer feedback)
- **Employment** (employer-initiated, evaluating applicant suitability)

You may use the informational interview to gain information about a job or company. You may use the performance interview to let others know how well or badly they are performing their current job. You might need to schedule a counseling interview after a potential employer finds a picture of you online from that pre-pandemic New Year's Eve. The skills that you will need, however, to get hired are those associated with the **employment interview**, which is why that interview type will be the focus of our discussion here.

Mediums: Online vs. in person vs. phone

Before launching into details of online interviewing, we should consider all interview mediums. Interviews in the modern era can happen via a variety of mediums – meaning that the communicated exchange of information can be scheduled to happen in various modes and settings (Auerbach, 2018; Berkelaar & Murphy, 2017). Interview mediums include: **1) Face-to-Face / In Person, 2) Telephone, and 3) Mediated Face-to-Face / Online Interviewing.** It is useful to know that you may begin an interview process in one medium (such as an online interview) and then be moved to another medium (in person or phone) as you advance through the interviewing process and depending on the locations of those with whom you need to interview.

Much of the interviewing information discussed in this chapter will be relevant to all three mediums and we will reference skills that are especially helpful to have in one or more of the specific mediums but our focus is on the **mediated face-to-face interview** process (AKA – online interviewing or video interviewing), which is where you will not be in the same room with the person interviewing you but are instead using any of a number of video-conferencing technologies. According to Ashira Prossack's (2019) article in *Forbes*, *How to Prepare for A Video Interview*, "Video interviews are starting to become the norm in the hiring process" to save travel time for applicants and company resources given to on-site interviews. Her article was written before COVID forced us all indoors but, the trend is likely to continue. The job search giant, Indeed (2021) argues that, "While COVID-19 made virtual interviewing a necessary practice, its popularity amongst employers is likely to stick post-pandemic. Virtual interviewing is convenient for employers as it allows for a more efficient interview process, eases scheduling conflicts, saves money and broadens the candidate pool."

What this means for you is that you had better be prepared for the online interview now and for most of your job seeking life. Sure, interviewers are still looking for many of the same elements that they would if you came in for an in-person interview but the technology itself presents challenges to effective communication. Internet connections fail, cameras result in a lack of eye contact, external noise can be different on each side of the mic resulting in unequal distractions... and the list goes on. What has not changed is that you must prepare and practice ahead for your online interview. No matter how many miles separate you; this mediated interaction is still the first step toward your career!

Prep (Before Your Online Interview)

"Have you worked on an Excel spreadsheet?" "What type of projects have you managed using Excel?" "How do you run a full macro in Excel and on what type of data set would you run one?" "Can you tell me about other database management systems that you have used?"

Do you see a trend here? Clearly, someone asking this particular group of questions wants to hire someone who is skilled at using Microsoft Excel. (And if you do not know how and when to run an Excel macro function then don't list Excel as a skill on your résumé.) Will your interviewer ask you these questions? What would you get asked in *your* interview? If you do not know then you have not yet taken the most important step for any interview... preparation. Preparation for online interviewing can be divided into two areas: technical preparation and interaction preparation.

Tips for Online Interviewing Tech-Prep

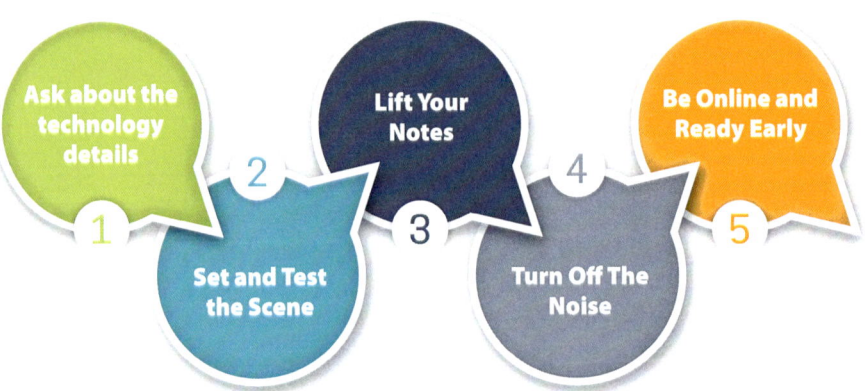

1. Ask about the technology details
2. Set and Test the Scene
3. Lift Your Notes
4. Turn Off The Noise
5. Be Online and Ready Early

Technical preparation is the part of online interviews that differs dramatically from traditional face-to-face interviews. Technology gives you more access and more options – but also complicates the interview process. You can find online any number of recommendations for technical preparation, but we have condensed those into the following "Tips for Online Interviewing Tech-Prep".

1. **Ask about the technology details:** What platform will be used? What is the length of the interview? Who will initiate the connection? What is the expected follow up if the tech fails – should you re-initiate or will they? (Ryan, 2020)

2. **Set (and test) the scene**: Are you familiar with the platform to be used? (If not, take a tutorial and practice with someone). Use your laptop and NOT YOUR PHONE because your connection will be more stable, your picture will be larger and have the right orientation, and you will have better access to platform tools (Forbes, 2021).

   a. Check your camera angle so that you are shown straight on rather than views of your ceiling. (This likely means placing your laptop on a box!) Be sure that you have tested it on the platform being used because what looks right on FaceTime might be distracting or 'off' when using Zoom.

   b. Remove background distractions. (Never have an unmade bed behind you – better yet – never have a bed in your scene. Blank walls or a tidy and classy room help to keep the focus on you and demonstrate the type of work that you will produce.) Get Fido out of the room and let others know to not disturb you.

   c. Have good lighting that removes odd shadows or reflections.

   d. Be cautious with Virtual Backgrounds: When you do not have a distraction free background, you might need a virtual one (JWU COE, 2021).
   Several sources suggest not using these backgrounds that can distract or fail but instead suggest choosing a room in your home and staging it for the interview (Flexjobs offers great tips for staging your room for an interview... and knowing what your background communicates to others!) (Pelta, 2020).

3. **Lift your notes:** Yes – you likely have notes about the company or reminders to yourself about good examples to offer but, if you are looking down at them then you break the connection with the interviewer so consider taping them just above your screen or camera or set them up on something next to your screen.

4. **Turn off the noise**: Find a location with little to no potentially loud distractions such as your roommate doing the dishes or traffic heard outside. Also, make sure that you do not have tech notifications going off such as your phone's ringer or email notifications (it's best to have those tabs off but if you need them open to receive links or documents from the employer during the interview then right click…. and mute that tab!).

5. **Be online and ready early:** "To be early is to be on time, to be on time is to be late, to be late is unacceptable." This old adage works well for the online interview setting. If you are late for an interview, your chance of getting the job is almost nil. Why? First of all, it implies a low value of the position. It reflects poorly on your future behavior if you do get hired. It is also disrespectful to the people who have set aside their time to get to know you. Technology can be tricky, so you want to be sure that before they come online — YOU are online. If your computer is on (not even open to the video platform) then you need to be on. Finish brushing your teeth, getting dressed, watching the *Today Show*, or searching for a pen prior to launching the software. You can have your video off until they say hello but assume that they can see you!

Now that you are technically prepared, give your attention to some of the preparation that cuts across medium or location issues — research and practice.

Research and Practice

Doing research into the company, the position, the industry, and potential questions can be a fun and enlightening process. What might you get asked in your interview? How creative are the questions? What does this company do to give back to the greater community? How can you contribute to their mission?

Start your research by considering the interview in general. Use any online search engine to search for "interview questions" and you will find literally thousands of ideas about what you might be asked. Basic questions such as, "Tell me about yourself" or "What is one of your weaknesses?" or "Do you prefer to work on your own or with a team?" will likely be asked regardless of the particular job because any employer would want to know. Compile a substantial list. Have at least 50 questions. Next, begin to search for potential questions that stem from the industry, the company, or job for which you will be interviewing. For instance, it is a fair bet to assume that you will be asked, "tell me what you know about our company" and should have learned as much as you can about the organization before your interview. You are also liable to be asked what you know about the industry (e.g., "How have accounting practices changed over the last decade?") and about the job (e.g., "Have you designed an in-house slide deck?"). Supplement your list of questions by asking people in the industry or by asking those who have been at their careers long enough to have conducted several interviews about what questions that they believe you might get.

Use the pages that follow to help you figure out answers to those questions — and then *practice.* Yes — you should practice for an interview in the same way that you practice for a sport. Know that it is rare to do well without trying as many techniques as possible and working on your endurance. Bilingual Content Producer for AL DÍA News Media, Lilia Zitlalit Ayllon, has the right idea. She says, "Having someone else ask me interview practice questions lets me hear myself out loud so I can get an idea of the best way to structure my answers by how they sound" (Sawyer, 2019). To prep for the questions, let's dive into how you can categorize and approach the types of interview questions that you get.

Types of Questions: Areas of Inquiry and Question Categories

Your list of questions (50 or more) might seem rather long and daunting to get through — until you break up your list questions into the categories in which most questions fall: include **expected, dreaded,** and **illegal**.

Expected questions are, well, expected. These are the questions that you are fairly certain that you will be asked because interviews naturally lend themselves to these questions. An expected question may stem from any of the below areas:

- **You** (your background, résumé, experience, characteristics, etc.)
- **The Industry** (the distinct grouping of enterprises in a particular field, country, region, or economy that are viewed collectively — such as Human Resources, Accounting, Education, etc.)
- **The Company** (or organization or nonprofit, etc.)
- **The Job/Position** (all details listed in the job description as well as the expected)

Consider the following general purpose, potentially expected questions and why they might have been asked. These questions and the indications of why they might be asked were drawn from a variety of sources (Doyle, 2019; Friedman, 2018; Peterson, n.d.).

- **You Example Question**: "Tell me about yourself." Employers do not want extensive history of your life. This is your chance to offer the well-crafted brand that you worked to develop in your résumé, online, and in support materials.

- **The Industry Example Question**: "What are your current salary expectations?" Remember that salary is different per industry and per job. Employers love to have you start this discussion (because hopefully your offer is low, and they can give it to you without you ever worrying about your higher value), however, this question is really only appropriate later in the interview process when you know that you are getting an offer. At that time, you should have more to go on that will link your worth to the position. Regardless, however, of when you get the question, remember that salary is only one part of the package. Ask for more information… and time (e.g., "I will really only be able to answer that when I have full information about health benefits, 401K, on-site offers such as parking, etc. Is there someone in HR who sends out an overview?" or "Now that I know that the job comes with specific benefits and responsibilities, I have an idea of the range. I would like to first hear what is most comfortable for your team and see how that fits for me.")

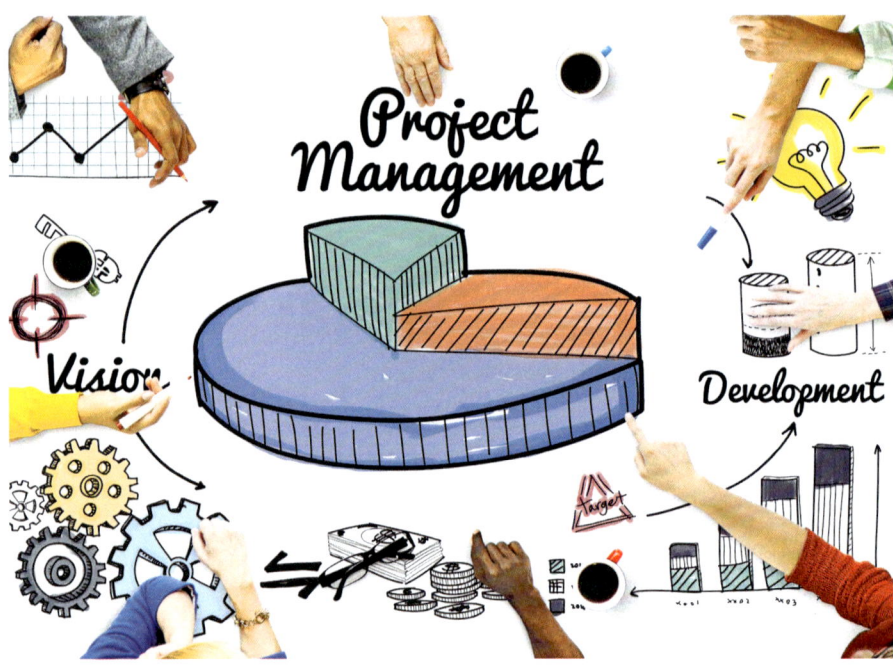

- **The Company Example Question**: "Why do you want to work for (us)?" Sub in the name of your potential company for the "us" part of the question because employers want to know what you know about *them* and what qualifications make you a good fit for *their* existing needs.
- **The Job/Position**: "Tell me about your most successful project management task." If you are applying to be a project manager... expect to get questions about project management. Whatever the job, expect that employers will ask you about your skills and abilities for every detail of the job advertisement. If you are to know Photoshop then you better have a project in mind that demonstrates your use of this software, etc. Employers are looking for specifics to gauge your idea of success. Frame your response in terms of your past employers' goals and be sure to link your strength in that area with the prospective company's goals. (Sidenote: Never take sole credit for any success that was not truly an individual effort.)

Unlike expected questions, a **dreaded question** will be unique to you. Let's say, for example, you get asked what type of tree you would be (a typical question to determine how you see yourself and if you can think metaphorically). Some candidates may dislike such abstract questions (i.e., they 'dread' them) while others see these questions as a fun challenge and, therefore, look forward to responding. A **dreaded question** is one that, for your own personal reasons, you are hoping that an interviewer will not ask. A good reason to identify a large set of your own personally dreaded questions is because you don't want to be caught off guard should they be asked. For instance, (and – again - drawn from the same above sources), the below questions might be dreaded by some and are drawn from examples that interviewers have actually asked.

- "**Why do you have so little experience?**" The tone of the question is off-putting and the phrasing you hear could be different but when you are new to your career, be ready for any version of this question. Employers are bound to wonder about your preparation for their advertised position. If you have not had an internship or past job or anything other than schoolwork on your application materials, then, yes, you will get asked about this.
- "**Tell me about your worst employer.**" Never badmouth a past employer. Employers want to test your tactfulness. In fact, negative talk about a current or past boss was

one of the top mistakes listed by hiring managers according to a Career Builder Survey (for review, see: Abbajay in the Harvard Business Review, 2018). If your last boss was a horrible person (or something less tactful), then focus on the challenging environment and what you learned from it.

- **"If you were a (insert animal or car or other inanimate object) what would you be?"** Employers want to know how well you know yourself – and that can be stressful. All of those random questions that compare you to animals, books, trees, and more are a means of challenging you. (No one really cares if you would be a redwood or pit bull or a chocolate chip cookie.) If you know yourself well then you may find the specific "what would you be" question less dreadful. Start with a statement about yourself and then identify the object that represents that self-concept (e.g., "I see myself as a team player who always helps both myself and others reach their goal. I know that dolphins work together on everything from finding food to identifying underwater explosives. I see myself just like that and hope that I can work with others here at your company to reach your goals…. and avoid those under water bombs!")

Expected questions are the ones that you are likely to get, and dreaded questions are the ones you hope you won't but for which you still to prepare. But what about those questions that you truly should not get? Too often, you will be asked illegal questions. In general, any question that allows an employer to evaluate you based upon criteria that does not pertain to the job is an **illegal question**. We offer the below information not as part of your legal education or to serve as a foundation for potential litigation. The intricacies of the law are not part of the preparation that we offer here. Instead, use the information below to determine when and how to address those questions that you know full well have absolutely nothing to do with how well you could do that job. If they have no bearing on the job, however, you might wonder why they get asked.

People ask illegal questions for three reasons: 1) they want to see how you will react, 2) they honestly want to know the answer, and 3) they are simply making conversation. Sometimes communicating through a computer can make people a bit more brazen in asking questions – the same way some students are more likely to ask professors questions via email that they would never ask in class (Alsharif, & Alyousef, 2017).

Strategic Ambiguity

Before offering up examples of illegal questions, consider this. All questions, even illegal questions, need a response. Silence is not an option (and this is not the time to pretend that your audio cut out). Neither is taking on a confrontational tone (not if you think you want the job). Instead, approach illegal questions strategically.

First, answer if, and only if, you feel comfortable being evaluated on your response. For example, you might be happy to answer, "Where did you get the artwork on the wall behind you?" or "Is that a Rice Husk cup you are using?" or "Is that your natural hair color?".

Second, if you do not feel comfortable answering, then use strategic ambiguity to *imply* an answer. **Strategic ambiguity** means giving the impression of having provided information even without offering a direct response (see: Levers of Persuasion, 2019). In this method, you will address what can be the "perceived" question – such as for the question: "Do you go on vacation with your family?" and you could reply, "I love family vacations – they bring people closer together. I personally would never take time off from work during deadlines or critical operations for a family trip." This is a means of addressing the potential concern of time away from work while not telling people your own private business or that you do take two weeks in Cape May with your family and plan to ask for time off. Even if the interviewer knows that you didn't answer the question, they are less likely to ask it again. But…. some people do.

Third, if strategic ambiguity didn't work or it confused the interviewer and they follow up by asking the question again, it is time to turn the tables and, very kindly and with an inquisitive nature, ask how subject pertains to the job (e.g., "I haven't been asked about politics during my interviews at other companies. Will politics be part of this job?")

Finally, if they ask again, it's time to let the interviewer know, in the most polite and respectful manner possible that you prefer not to answer. The bottom line is that your answers should, whenever possible, draw the discussion back to the employer's needs for the specific job at that specific time because the more you are able to do so – the more effective you will be.

Remember that you are interviewing the employer as much as they are interviewing you. If the person on the other side of the computer screen makes you feel uncomfortable during the interview, then they are not likely to be the greatest professional colleague. At this point, you know *why* people ask you questions; you know that categorizing potential questions helps better understand why they were asked but, now you need to know *how* to answer those questions.

Organized and Specific Responses

Employer: "Tell me about yourself."
Interviewee: "Well, I'm a junior at the local college majoring in Finance."
Employer (to themselves): Oh jeez…. one of a hundred.

If an employer needed no more information than what is on your résumé then they would not bother to set up your online interview. When someone has gone through the trouble to make arrangements to meet you, then your role is to provide them with enough feedback that they can evaluate your fit with their company. Online interviews may be more convenient and give us greater access to one another, but they also limit our interactions (e.g., no going to lunch with job candidates or walking them through the office to see how they interact with the whole team) and put greater importance on what we say. To give employers a strong sense of who you are, you need to have responses that are organized and detailed.

Interview responses, as with speeches, that have no organization are difficult to follow and recall. For this reason, most job search sites have acronyms for how you should organize your answers to interview questions (for example, some include STAR, PAR, SAR, S-PAR, etc.) (Doyle, 2019). These abbreviations are all just means of doing the same thing…. helping you offer concise but clear information. For our purposes, PAR (Problem-Action-Results) is the most useful response organization to apply in the online interview setting.

PAR stands for Problem, Action, Results. Not every question asks you to address a problem, but most do want you to address a:

(P) SPECIFIC problem or situation that you faced then an

(A) action or steps that you took to manage the situation, and

(R) detailed, precise results of your action.

The example below shows you how all of this can happen in just a few sentences!

> **"What major challenges and problems did you face in getting your Business Management degree? How did you handle them??**
>
> P: "The workload was especially difficult because expectations in this major are so high and extremely realistic for post-graduation work. The most challenging course that I took was Personal Sales (BSM 480) with Professor Taylor Kreps."
>
> A: "While their course was demanding (with a Corporate Research Project, three speeches including an Elevator Speech and two CEO interviews), I found that working efficiently and using a calendar to map out my workflow helped me to be proficient and manage the workload. Plus, the class was really fun when I wasn't stressed out about meeting deadlines.
>
> R: "This tactic must have worked because I received a high grade in the course (a B+) along with a really wonderful letter of recommendation from Professor Kreps, which I actually included in my application packet for this position. I know that from my degree and classes like theirs that lots of projects is the professional norm for this industry and enjoying the work makes all the difference."

Answers like these make staring into the computer screen enjoyable on both sides. You can think of your answers like mini stories that you get to tell, and the interviewer is more easily captivated by a narrative (Green & Brock, 2000; Green & Sestir, 2017). Anyone can talk about, for instance, their "aptitude for leadership" when asked about a good quality, but someone who can offer a short story about how she or he took on a leadership role in a specific club or class project and then turned that role into an opportunity, well,... now *that* is impressive!

Asking Questions Back

Effective interviewers will give you, at some point, an opportunity to ask questions. Remember that the interview is a conversation, a two-way interaction, and that you should be prepared to ask questions throughout the process or (at the very least) when asked. This is your chance to show your interest in the company and see how well you will fit in their organization. Most industry sources recommend asking questions from among the categories here (see: Bond, 2018, Gillett, 2018):

- **About the position:** Including questions such as – Was the position newly created? If not, how long has the position been vacant? How often and through what means will my job performance be evaluated?
- **About the company**: Including questions such as – How is job performance evaluated? What are the company's strategies to remain competitive and what is my role in that?
- **About environment**: Including questions such as – Was the predecessor promoted or did s/he leave? What is the typical workday or week like?
- **About expectations**: Including questions such as – What qualities would the ideal candidate have, and what skills and abilities would go above and beyond expectations?
- **About the timeline**: Rather than set yourself up for weeks of agony, be sure to ask about the timeline for making job offers. If the hiring manager says that they still have 3 weeks of interviewing to do then you know not to worry if you hear nothing for 2 weeks. If they said 48 hours, then you will want to follow up once that time has passed. Asking about the timeline helps lessen your anxiety and increases their accountability; however, this should never be your *only* question. When they ask if you have questions and you seem to care nothing for additional information from any of the areas listed above but only ask about the timeline then you will come off as self-centered, which is NOT what you want.
- **About where to send mail**: We will give more details in the following pages but, take at least one moment to ask for a good mailing address for those interviewing you. With so many people working from home, you may not know where to send requested hard copies of documents or a hard copy thank you note. Be sure to ask – and if you ask for this address then be sure to use it.

Be careful. You do not yet have the job so questions about what the company can do to adjust to your specific desires and needs (or the salary that you want) should be held until you have an offer. Questions let people know that you have thought about the actual job and not just the interview. So, ask questions… and do it with confidence!

What They See and Hear

Because we are talking about online interviewing, we should address the obvious. Online interviewing is visual by nature. When your camera is not on, you have a photo of yourself broadcast to the group (or if you don't, you should!). What are you wearing in that photo? What about once the camera is on? Do you appear to be taking the interview seriously by showing appropriate dress? Do you seem comfortable and confident in the kind of clothes that you will be wearing everyday once in the office – or working remotely? Are you distracting with a bracelet, watch, or chair that makes noise? Do those enormous headphones look ridiculous and distracting??! Do you look interested – but sound annoyed? What the interviewer sees and hears is critical to your success.

Attire

What "professional attire" means is quite different in different industries, different companies, and even for different roles at the same company. It is no longer possible to just "wear a dark suit" and you're good. Just like with the research that you did finding questions for your PAR question-response preparation, you must research what to wear and how that look appears once on camera (Ryan, 2021).

The person interviewing you is looking for visual similarity in interviewees. Some things are beyond our control. For instance, psychologists have long known that we are more drawn to people who look more like us (Brogaard, 2015). We cannot control our physical characteristics but, there are some things – such as what we wear – that are within our control. "It's the ultimate sartorial irony: Less restrictive dress codes were supposed to make life more comfortable for everyone. Instead, with the old rules gone, many people are in a state of dress-down confusion." Management consultant and CNBC contributor, Suzy Welch, explains that "the workplaces of today may be less strict about attire, but there are still guidelines…. The burden is on (the applicant) to pick appropriate attire for wherever your job search takes you" (Connley, 2018).

In terms of general pointers on attire (that might not be the case for *every* workplace), consider how your attire communicates. For instance:

- More formal attire is more respected: young professionals prefer a more casual atmosphere, but society still links higher levels of professional attire with higher authority (Connley, 2018).
- Backlash from too casual attire is increasing; companies who have seen too casually dressed employees are reacting by creating and enforcing specific policies (Gustashaw, 2019).
- Formality is specific to industries: what is considered casual in one industry will be considered too casual in another industry (Huen, 2019).
- Less make-up signals confidence: moderate cosmetics helped women be perceived as healthier and more confident than those without (Grant, 2018).

If you do not know what specifically will be appropriate for the company and employees with whom you are interviewing, then do some research. Go to the office to look (if the office is open to the public and the work is not remote). See if you can subtly swing by – perhaps just to go in the lobby if you can. You might also get a sense of the mood and formality of the office by looking at the company's marketing materials including executive and employee profile pictures. You can also ask someone who works there or has been to the office or worked with the company. Once you have found the right level of formality and tone – check to see if the outfit shows well on camera. A long jacket might bunch up oddly around your shoulders while you sit or jewelry that is fantastic in person could be too distracting when only your head and shoulders are seen on the screen. What would be far too tight of a shirt to wear in person could appear to be tailored and conservative online. Practice – and ask!

Answer Tone and Nonverbal

Clothing is not the only thing that will set the tone of your interview. Your voice and nonverbal communication also set a tone. Have you ever watched a newscaster talk about something awful but with a big smile? It's like they have a complete disconnect from the story. Watching it can feel awkward and unsettling. The same is true for your online interview. *How* you say things will matter more because there are fewer interactional cues for the interviewer to use for interpretation. If your 'thinking face' comes across as "resting (bleep) face" then you can alienate your audience. Your vocal tone, nonverbal communication, and what you will wear **really** matter so you must be at the top of your game!

Before the big day, practice (and record if you can) your interview to see how your voice, attire, and nonverbal communication will send messages. Use Lilia Zitlalit Ayllon's advice to have someone sit with you to ask you those 50 questions that you found and see how you answer them. Watch the video back to determine if your voice was inviting or if you need a different color lipstick. Ask yourself what your facial expressions communicate. Did you show interest with nonverbal cues? Did you smile in an authentic way that reaches your eyes? Did you make eye contact, which means looking at the camera rather than the face of the interviewers on your screen? Did you angle your camera to capture your gestures so that the visual is more engaging?

Now when you turn the camera on and are waiting for the others to join the session, you may be nervous, (which is natural) but you will not be unprepared. You will likely have a great interaction with those on the other end of the camera and the time will move quickly. Once you finish your interview and close the Zoom or other platform, you might think that you now are finished and should just wait for that "you got the job!" email. We aren't there yet. You still need to communicate once the interview is over — and some organizations say that this step is the final evaluation of their candidates.

Post-Interview Interaction

Say thank you. Your mom has probably been telling you this for years and now is when it will really pay off – literally! The most crucial element of your follow-up is a thank you letter. As a rule of thumb, if the employer uses email to contact you, it is acceptable to use the same medium to communicate back during the process and you can email an appreciative note back to everyone who you saw while online, but a hard copy thank-you is what will help you stand out more than anyone else.

Old-fashioned, hand-written letters are still preferable to email alone and certainly preferable to not sending any type of thank you (Segelin, 2017). Jessica Liebman, executive managing editor at *Business Insider,* writes, "I've been hiring people for 10 years, and I still swear by a simple rule: If someone doesn't send a thank-you email, don't hire them" (Lipman, 2019). If you remembered to ask for a mailing address as one of your final questions, then you are ready to go. Grab that classy looking stationery (not a card from the birthday section at Target – but you can buy inexpensive, tasteful stationery there). Keep your note short and spelled correctly. Mention something specific and interesting that was discussed during your interview and then reiterate your interest in the position. Most importantly, mail this letter immediately, preferably on the same day. Then be ok waiting a bit before reaching out again.

It can seem like an eternity since you had your interview, and you might want to reach out the next day to ask them how you did but... hold up. A status inquiry is important – especially in these times where we are all so distant with online interviews and remote working positions. You absolutely should follow up and may even need to do so more than once as long as you give the hiring manager a realistic amount of time. We mentioned earlier that asking for a timeline is critical so wait until that time has hit or just before it to follow up by email or phone. If you don't hear back then wait about five to eight business days before another follow up. Certainly, make sure you do not hassle the person before the specified date that they gave you at the end of the interview especially since, even if they have made a decision, it can take time on their part to finalize how to move forward. When you do follow-up, be sure that you are polite and not pushy. It may take several follow-up calls to get your ideal boss to call you back for the ideal job (Buj, 2018). Stay positive and stay on it!

Looking Back

You have the ability to interview well in an online or virtual setting. Be confident! Be composed (and intelligible and direct). You now know the type of interview that you had (an employment interview) and that several of the recommendations here apply to all interview mediums but are specifically important for the online interview. You have read about necessary preparations, how to keep organized in an online interview setting, and how to answer questions effectively. We even covered the tone and nonverbal strategies that help to engage others in a virtual interview setting as well as the critical follow-up efforts that you should make. Hopefully these will help you build your confidence and secure your ideal job.

Remember that technology has changed so much from your parents' time interviewing that they may not be able to guide you through the process as well as they had hoped that they could. Reading from the sources here and learning applications in your classes will position you well. Still need to wrap your brain around all of this? *The Harvard Business Review* offers a quick checklist for your online interview that touches on each of the areas we have detailed about (https://hbr.org/2020/06/how-to-nail-a-job-interview-remotely). Print it out. Have it at home. Use it to get ready. And... happy interviewing!

References

Green, M. C., & Brock, T. C. (2000). The role of transportation in the persuasiveness of public narratives. Journal Of Personality and Social Psychology, 79(5), 701. Chicago.

Green, M. C., & Sestir, M. (2017). Transportation theory. The International Encyclopedia of Media Effects, 1-14.

Gustashaw, M. (2019, March 15). Business casual: These are the new rules of office dressing. GQ Magazine. https://www.gq.com/story/new-rules-of-business-casual-2019.

Huen, E. (2019, May 19). What 'business casual' really means in 2019. Forbes. https://www.forbes.com/sites/eustaciahuen/2019/05/09/businesscasual/#3996582c2e81.

Indeed. (2021, May 10). How to succeed in a virtual interview. https://www.indeed.com/career-advice/interviewing/virtual-interview.

JWU COE - Johnson & Wales University College of Education. (2021, May 3). 15 tips for acing an online job interview. https://online.jwu.edu/blog/15-tips-acing-online-job-interview.

Landry, L. (2018, October 3). 9 tips for mastering your next virtual interview. Harvard Business School Online. https://online.hbs.edu/blog/post/virtual-interview-tips.

Levers of Persuasion. (2019, April 01). Strategic ambiguity. https://leversofpersuasion.com/strategic-ambiguity/.

Lipman, V. (2019, April 08). How important is it to send a 'thank you' after a job interview? Forbes. https://www.forbes.com/sites/victorlipman/2019/04/08/how-important-is-it-to-send-a-thank-you-after-a-job-interview/#73567b877505.

Pelta, R. (2020, August 13). What your video interview background really says about you. Flexjobs Blog. https://www.flexjobs.com/blog/post/video-interview-background-really-says/.

Peterson, T. (n.d.). 100 top job interview questions-be prepared for the interview. Monster. https://www.monster.com/career-advice/article/100-potential-interview-questions.

Prossack, A. (2019, April 26). How to prepare for a video interview. Forbes. https://www.forbes.com/sites/ashiraprossack1/2019/04/26/video-job-interview-tips/#a52167059782

Ryan. R. (2020, March 10). 7 Tips on How to Succeed In An Online Job Interview. Forbes. https://www.forbes.com/sites/robinryan/2020/03/10/7-tips-on-how-to-succeed-in-an-online-job-interview/?sh=7c93d48553c7.

Sawyer, J. K. (2019). Business Talk (2nd ed.). Philadelphia Press. (pp. 179).

Segelin, A. (2017, May 15). Why you must send a thank you note after every job interview. Fortune. http://fortune.com/2017/05/15/job-interview-thank-you-note/.

A

Abbreviations, 154, 159–160
about.com, 55
Accept consequences of our own communication, NCA credo, 106
Action, 82, 92, 94
Active audience, audience type, 34
Active listening, 25
Adaptation, and audience centered speech, 31
Adrenaline and cortisol. *See* Fight or flight response
Affect displays, in online communication, 130–131
Agenda for meetings, 171
American Society for Prevention of Cruelty to Animals, emotion in ads, 85
Americans with Disabilities Act (ADA), live captioning and subtitles, 117
Analogy, definition of, 95
Angelou, Maya, "Words are things," 38–39
Anger, 88, 91
Anti-Slavery Bugle, Sojourner Truth's speech, 1
Anxiety. 135–147; *See also* Communication apprehension; De-stress; Glossophobia; Stress
Appearance, in online communication, 123–124, 125–126
Application and desktop sharing, useful during team meetings, 169
Argument. 97, 98, 99, 100-102
Aristotle's *Art of Rhetoric* 14, 29, 30, 40–41, 85–86, 89
Articulate words and practice hard words, for online communication, 132
Artifacts, removal of for virtual interaction, 127
Ask a question, visual answer, 73–74
Ask for current resume, 183
ask.com, 55
Aspiration, 88, 91-92
Asynchronous communication, 2
AT&T's picture phone technology, 3
Attention, evoking emotion as part of Monroe's Motivational Sequence, 92
Attitudinal inherency, 101
Attitudes, beliefs, and values of audience, 33
Audience
    analysis of, *see* Audience analysis
    attitudes, beliefs, and values of, 33
    characteristics of determine content, style, length, and delivery of presentation, 13
    definition of, 30
    demographics, *see* Audience demographics
    electronic surveys before meeting, 172
    keep in mind during preparation of speech and presentation, 154
    and knowledge of speech topic, 43
    motivations of, 33
    multi-tasking of during virtual presentations, 7
    and my goals in selecting audience-centered topic, 42
    respect for, 114–118
    types of 34–35
Audience analysis, 29-38, 69, 90, 181
Audience centered, 30–34, 42, 86
Audience demographics, 42, 43, 86-87
Audience disruptions, handling of, 43
Audience engagement, 16, 23
Audience expectations, 42, 43
Audience feedback, 43, 44
Audience incentive, 42
Audience members, identify with and find common ground with, 116
Audience needs, selecting audience-centered topic, 42
Audience reaction to speaker, 41
Audience receptiveness, selecting audience-centered topic, 42
Audience research, sets stage for audience-centered speech, 32–33
Audience respect, accountability and responsibility, 114
Audience size, 33, 34, 36
Audience survey, on knowledge of speaker's topic, 52
Audience values, definition of, 33
Audience-centered topic, 42
Audio on web platform, 168
Audio playback of voice, Edison's device-asynchronous, 2
Audiovisual clip, to reengage audience, 41
Audiovisual communication, 3, 6
Authenticity, 29, 42
Ayllon, Lilia Zitlalit, 199

Back-up plan for visual aid problems, 161
Background, for virtual interaction, 126–127
Background noise, avoid for online communication, 127

INDEX

Be honest, on your intentions for speaking, 117
Bell, Alexander Graham, 2
"Before anything else, preparation is the key to success," 162

Best practices in communication, 116
Bias, avoid in choosing material, 58
Blogs, citations required for, 64
Blue color, not for slide background, 156
Body, of speech, 150
Body language, 3. *See also* Kinesics
Body position during speech, 41
Body posture, and confidence, 143–144
Body under stress, release, redirect, reframe, 142–144
Bookcase, for virtual interaction, 127
Boolean operators, 54
Brain-labeling responses, 140
Breathe, to de-stress, 142
Brief example, 61, 62
Bubble technique, visualization to de-stress, 143
Burke, Kenneth, 116
Bush versus Clinton debate, emotional disconnect versus empathy, 29, 30
Business causal, for online events, 125

C

Calendly, invite people to meetings, 172
Camera angle to see hands, for on online communication, 130
Camera lens, focus for online communication, 126
"Cancel culture," 111
Cannon, Walter, on flight or fight response, 137–138
Captive audience, audience type, 34
Categorial organizational pattern of speeches, 81–82
Ceremonial presentations, 17
Chair, for online communication, 128–129
Challenges after speech, 17
Channel or medium, delivery mode, 6
Character, as narrative element, 94
Chat, 6, 169
Chocolate slide, 151
Chronemics, time in nonverbal communication, 35
"Chunking" information, 65, 66–67
Citation of sources, 64
Claims of fact, truth or falsity, 98
Claims of policy, 98
Claims of value, 97
Clapping, 130
Climate change, Gore v. Bush campaign, 39–40
Clothing, 124-125, 207, 208

Clues to a Great Story, Andrew Stanton, 89
Clydesdale horse, emotion of ads, 85
Colbert, Stephen, "Truthiness" defined, 60
Colloquiums, defined, 179
Commencement speech, 13
Communication, modern models of, 6
Communication apprehension, 135, 140-146
Communication climate of caring and mutual understanding, NCA credo, 106
Communication process, core components of, 5
Communication skills, improvement in, 120
Communicators, older communication models, 5–6
Compensatory justice, defined, 91
Comprehension of speech, how much information, 65
Computer-assisted communication, and digital presentations, 30
Conclusion to speech, 77–79, 150
Condemn communication that degrades people, NCA credo, 106
Confidence-boosting exercises, 140–146
Connotations and denotations, naming our emotions to harness them, 145
Content, 24, 159
Context for speech, occasion or time, 33
Controversial messages, caution with, 114
Convenience and access to information, 110
Convention headliner's speech, 1–2
Conversation starters, 20–21
Copy and paste, and copyright violations, 109
Copyleaks.com, copyright-takedown requests, 108–109
Copyright, and images on web, 64; *See also* Fair use laws
Cost effectiveness, virtual events preferred, 9
Counseling interviews, 194
Courageous expression of personal convictions, NCA credo, 106
Courbert, Stephen, monologue to persuade, 97
COVID-19, 4, 193-194, 195
Credibility, 29, 43, 111, 117, 118
Credo for Ethical Communication, by National Communication Association (NCA), 89, 105–108
Crossed arms, avoid for online communication, 129–130
Cuddy, Dr. Amy, body posture and positive evaluations, 143–144
Cultural communication competency, 44
Currency of information, 59
Curry, Stephen, 63

Data, factual and cross-referenced, 111
Data visualization, McCandless, David, 153
Databases, 56, 57
De-stress, breathing exercises, 142
Delivery mode, channel or medium, 6
Delivery of speech, elements of, 16
Demographic research, and audience-centered speech, 31
Desensitization, 141
Digital communication, definition of, 4, 5
Digital hand, 23
Digital Media Law Project, 112
Digital presentations, 44, 69-83, 110–111
Direct quote, in testimony, 63
Disagreement, need to verify claims, 111
Distractions, 6, 21, 26, 43
Diverse audiences, speaker dialogue with, 44
Diversity, and ethical communication, 89, 106, 119
Do not read from prepared text, for online communication, 132
Dobrin et al., on purpose of visual aid, 149–150
Document sharing, on virtual meeting technology, 168
Dreaded question in interview, 201–202
Dress codes, and online interview garb, 207–208
Dressing, for online appearance, 124–125

Edison, Thomas, record and playback of human voice, 2
Effect-Cause-Action, for conclusion, 83
Effective listening, 26
ehow.com, 55
Election polls, statistics with serious limitations, 61
Elsevier, open-access journals, 55
Emotion, for argument, 85-102
Emotion-evoking language, imagery, 93–94
Employment interviews, 194
Energy-release suggestions, fight or flight response, 143
Entertainment speech, educate and motivate audience, 31–32, 39
Environment or location of speech, setting considerations, 34
Ethical communication, 89, 105-106
Ethical listening, 116, 119
Ethical research, 116
Ethical responsibilities, of speakers to be accurate and honest, 58

Ethics, 105–120
Ethos, 37, 111; see also Aristotle's *Art of Rhetoric*
Eulogy's purpose, 36
Evidence, 58–64
Examples, 61, 62–63, 151
Exchange of meaning, message from speaker and feedback from recipients, 6
Existential inherency, 101
Exit interviews, 194
Expectations--misreading of, speaker challenges with audience, 43
Expected outcome of speech, 18
Extended example, 62–63
External HD camera, 126
Eye contact, 6, 130–131

Face-to-face, *versus* virtual presentations, 13–27, 21–23
Facebook posts, citations required for, 64
Facial expressions, 130–131
Facial hair and online communication, 126
Facilitator, to manage hindrances, 7
Fair use law, 157
    in academic setting, 112
Fallacies, defined, 114
Fallon, Jimmy, monologue to persuade, 97
Fear, 88, 90, 114–115
Fear appeals, use of, 115, 116
Feedback, 6, 40
Feel the Fear and Do It Anyway, 135, 144
Fight or flight response, 87, 88, 137, 142, 143
File links, as visual aid for virtual presentations, 150
First impression, online, 124
Flip chart, as visual aid, 150
Floyd and Canton, on colloquiums, 179
Follow-up, 16–17, 174–175
Font in visual presentations, 158
Forums, defined, 179
Freedom of expression, NCA credo, 106

Gage, Frances Dana, record of Sojourner Truth's speech, 1
Gestures, 129-130
Gingerich, Newt, speaker overwhelmed audience, 29
Glossophobia, 135–137
Goal in appealing to emotion, 89–90
Goals for audience, 58

INDEX

Goals of meetings, 170
Goals for speaker, 58
Good person speaking well, 117
Google Chrome, 167
Google Hangouts, for professional purposes, 194
Google Meet, 150
Google Scholar, 55
Google searches per year, 53
Google Slides, works on web- and server-based platforms, 172
Gore, Al, climate change, 39–40
GoToMeeting, for web browser meetings, 167
Grab attention, arouse curiosity of audience, 153
Great communicators' traits, 29
Green screen, 126
Grievance interviews, 194
Guide to Public Speaking, 151

Hair and online communication, 126
Handouts, as visual aid for in-person presentations, 150
Harvard Business School, recognizing stress and relabeling it, 145
Hearing, different from listening, context, 23–25
Hecklers, handling of, 43
High-power poses, and positive evaluation, 143–144
Hindrances, 7
Hostile audience, 35
How much information for comprehension of speech?, 65, 66
Howard, Dr. Sheena, Speaker, Message, Audience Cycle (SMAC), 113
Human resources or publications departments, source for images or graphics, 158
Human voice, first record of, 2
Humor, to reengage audience, 41
Humorous story, at beginning of speech, 75–76

"I Have a Dream" speech," 3, 93
Illegal question in interview, 202-204
Illustration real or hypothetical, at beginning of speech, 76
Images, 64, 158,
Inattentive audience, reengagement of, 41
Inclusivity, 107, 112–114
Indicate important information, in speech delivery, 16
Information, 52–65

Information gap, between speaker and audience, 51–52
Information gathering, 67
Information Society, 52
Informational interviews, 194
Informative speech, 17, 31
Inherency of debate, actual situation and status quo, 101
Instagram photos, citations required for, 64
Intended plagiarism, 110–112
Interactive audiovisual communication, AT&T's picture phone technology, 3
Internal distractions, to effective listening, 26–27
Internet, web-enhanced personal devices commonplace, 3
Interrogation interviews, 194
Interview mediums, 195
Interview questions, 198–207
and Problem, Action, Results (PAR), 204–205

Interviewing, *See* Online interviewing
Interviews, 35, 123, 194-195
Introduction of speech, 73, 75–77, 82, 150
Involuntary audience, audience type, 35

Jargon, 95, 96
Jewelry for online communication, 126
Job interview, 13, 210
Joke, at beginning of speech, 75–76
JSTOR, 56

"Keep calm and carry on," British World War II poster, 142
Kennedy, John F., quote from, 64, 75
Keywords and memorable phrases, 132
Kimmel, Jimmy, monologue to persuade, 97
Kinesics, 41, 128–129
King, Dr. Martin Luther, "I Have a Dream" speech, 3, 93
Konigsburg, E. L., 5 minutes of planning, 53
Krane, Dr. Elliot, *Meaning of Chronic Pain,* 95
Kristof, Nicholas, 65

LaBon, Gustave, on power of words and images, 37
Language to evoke emotion, 92–96
Laptop presentation, on Smartphone, 10
Large audience, and misinterpretation, 35

Lehrman, Sally, listening for diversity, 119, 120
libgen.li, free information source, 53
Liebman, Jessica, thank-you letter important, 210
Lighting, 6, 127
Limbic system, 87, 88, 137–140. See also Fight or flight
Listeners' recall, primacy-recency effect, 67
Listening, 23-25, 119-120; See also Active listening
Live captioning and subtitles, for Americans with Disabilities Act (ADA) compliance, 117
Lizard brain, in stress, 137–140. See also Stress
Location, 36, 127
Logos, 111, 117; See also Aristotle's Art of Rhetoric

M

Magical number 7, Plus or Minus 2, 65
Main idea, discreetness, 70
Manipulation, definition of, 89
Manner, as narrative element of how characters approach conflict, 94
Marconi, Guglielmo, invented wireless communication, 2
Martinville, Edouard-Leon Scott de, first record of human voice, 2
Mayo Clinic, 63, 136
McCabe, Dr. Donald and International Center for Academic Integrity, 108–109
McCandless, David, data visualization, 153
McCroskey, Dr. James, communication apprehension, 135
Media, as visual aid for virtual presentations, 150
Mediated communication, definition, 30
Mediated face-to-face interview; See also Online interviewing
Meeting host's roles, 171-172

Meetings, 170, 171
Meme, Bernie Sanders' campaign and sparrow, 38
Messaging, importance of emotions to, 102
Microsoft Live Meeting, server-based platforms, 168
Microsoft PowerPoint, works on web- and server-based platforms, 172
Microsoft Teams, 194
Microsoft's PowerPoint, common corporate presentation software, 150
Moderating virtual panels and presentations, 179–191
Monotone, avoidance of, 132

Monroe, Alan H., *Monroe's Principles of Speech*, 92
Monroe's Motivational Sequence, 82, 83, 91–92
Multitasking myth, 27
Mute, 7, 113

N

Narrative. 39, 61, 94-95, See also Extended example
National Communication Association (NCA), *Credo for Ethical Communication*, 89, 105–108
Need, 82, 92
Nerves. See Anxiety
Networking, purpose of, 20–21
New York Times, database, 56
Nieuwfof, Cary, more work to be clear than confusing, 70
Noise, deterrence of, 7
Nonverbal communication, 40–41, 44, 128, 208–209
"Not," as Boolean operator, 54
Note taking, encourages active listening, 25

O

Obama, Barack, on global climate disruption, 39–40
Objectives of meetings, defined, 170
Occasion for speech, eulogy, 36
Online calendar tools, invite people to meetings, 172
Online communication, 4, 107, 123–147
Online environment, listening in, 119–120
Online information, finding of, 51–67
Online interviewing, 193–211. See Interviewing
Online listening sessions, goal of, 20
Online reputation, compromise of, 110–111
Online speech, 31-34
Open-access journals, 55
Opinion to persuade, argument, 97
"Or," as Boolean operator, 54, 55
Oral citations, on images in visual aids, 64
Oral reports, for group presentations, 179
Oratory preservation, in mid-nineteenth century, 1–2
Organizational patterns of speeches, 80–82
Outcome or resolution, as narrative element of how characters approach conflict, 94
Outcomes of speech, know in advance, 14
Outdoor speaking, need amplification of speaker, 34
Outline of speech, 71-72, 153

INDEX

Oxford Dictionary of Quotations, 75
Oxford University Press, open-access journals, 55
Oxygen, antidote to anxiety, 142

Panel, 179–188
Panel monitor checklist, 187–188
Panel presentations, 179
Panel speaker selection, 182
Panelists, 182–183, 188-190
Paralanguage, 40, 131–132. *See also* Rhythm, Volume and rate of speech
Paralinguistic cues, in virtual presentations, 25
Parallelism, in speech organization, 70
Paraphrase, rather than quote, 64
Passive audience, as audience type, 34
Pathos, 89, 88-90. 111, 117; *See also* Aristotle's *Art of Rhetoric*
Pauses in speaking, 132–133
Peer-reviewed academic journal articles, 112
Peer-reviewed databases, 55
Performance interviews, 194
Persuasive presentations, 17
Persuasion, 29-30
Persuasive speaking, 37
Persuasive speech, 14, 31, 83
Pets during virtual interaction, 127
Phobia. *See* Anxiety; Glossophobia
Physical discomfort, distraction to effective listening, 26
Physiological changes to emotions, 87–88
Pitch modulation, 40
Plagiarism, 65, 107–112
Plagiarist defined, 108
Plan policy change, who and how, 101
Plan speech, 14-15, 69
Plot, as narrative element, 94
Podium, for formal speech, 40–41
Polarization of speaker, speaker challenges with audience, 43
Policy update or change, speech to get audience to do something, 19
Political campaigns, language use in, 37–38
Polling, 169, 172
Positioning of strongest evidence, for comprehension of speech, 65
Posture, for online communication, 128–129
Powder to avoid face's shine on online communication, 126
Practice answering interview questions, 199
Practice speech, with notes and visual aids, 161–162
Preparation for speech, key to success, 9, 16, 162

Pre-recorded presentation, on video conferencing platform, 150
Presentation, in speech delivery, 16
Presentation software, 150
Presentations, 160–161, 172–173
Presenters at meeting, receive meeting goals and objectives, 171
Presidential campaign of 2016, language used in, 37–38
Prestige testimony, 63–64
Preview body of presentation, to help listeners stay on track, 77
Primacy-recency effect, helps listeners recall, 67
Primary sources, definition of, 52
Problem, Action, Results (PAR), interview questions response, 204–205
Professional associations, publications of, 55–56
Professional communication, requires thought and practice, 133
Project Gutenberg, digitizing of books, 53
Project lead. *See* Meeting host
Promote access to communication resources, and opportunities and NCA credo, 106
Prossack, Ashira, "How to Prepare for a Video Interview," 195
Public opinion polling, and Survey Monkey, 45–48
Public sources, citations required for, 64
Public speaking fear. *See* Anxiety; Glossophobia
Purpose of speech, guides preparation, 17

Qualitative and quantitative content, content, 159
Qualitative surveys, diverse types of feedback, 45
Quantitative surveys, provide hard data, 45
Question, to jolt audience through use of relevant query, 75
Question and answer portion of speech, 16–17, 40, 185–187
Questions about job or position in interview, 201
Questions of job seekers at interview, 206–207
Quotations, 63, 75

Radio signals, Marconi, 2
Re-using presentations, cautions about, 158
Record yourself, listen for pauses, 133
Recording, 169–170
Reference slide, for speech, 64
Rehearsal of speech, timing and flow, 16
Relabel and rename stress, use thinking brain, 144–146

Relate to audience, What's in it for me? (WIFM), 76–77
Release, redirect, reframe, for body under stress, 142–144
Relevance of information, analysis of, 60
Renaming physiological response as energy, directs energy toward presentation, 145
Reputable sources, 112
Research, 16, 53–54, 69, 151
Research company interviewing you, 198–199
Researching online information, 51–67
Resharing news, intended plagiarism, 110
Respecting the message, ethics and online communication, 107
Respecting your audience, ethics and online communication, 107
Respecting yourself, ethics and online communication, 107
Responsible speech goals, 114
Retaliatory justice, defined, 91
Rhetorical question, 41, 74
Rhythm of speech, Aristotle on, 40
Ring lighting, for online communication, 126
Robinson, Marius, Sojourner Truth's speech in *Anti-Slavery Bugle*, 1, 2
Roosevelt, Franklin Delano, on Pearl Harbor attack, 2
Rule of Three, for categorial organizational pattern of speeches, 81–82

S

Salary question in interview, 200
Sales video call, appearance during, 123
Sanders, Bernie, campaign of, 38
Satire, to reengage audience, 41
Satisfaction, evoking emotion as part of Monroe's Motivational Sequence, 92
Scale model as visual aid, 150
sci-hub, free information source, 53
Science Direct, for open-access journals, 55
Screen, competition for your attention, 154
Screen and reader-friendly options, ADA compliance, 117
Search engines, 56–57
Search terms, strategies for, 53–55
Search tools, best available, 55
Secondary sources, definition of, 52
Selecting technology, 166–167
Self-disclosure, 41, 43
Self-reflection, and audience centered speech, 31
Self-respect, display credibility, integrity, and accountability, 117

Server-based platforms, 168
SET, statistics, examples, and testimony, 66
Setting, as narrative element, 94
Setting the stage for presentation, 6, 17
Shared space, and virtual interaction, 127
Sharing information, opinions, and feelings on significant choices, NCA credo, 106
Short phrases on visual aids, 154
Significance of debate, quantitative and qualitative ignorance, 100
Situational audience analysis, size and time, 35
Skill or knowledge acquisition, 20
Slides, 153-156, 158-160
Small audience, and misinterpretation, 35
Snapping, on online communication, 130
Social anxiety disorder, 136-137
Social justice movements, anger based, 91
Social media, boosts plagiarism, 108
Social sciences database searches, JSTOR, 56
Solvency, advantages of planned change, 101
Sound, volume of, 40
Source evaluation, 58–59
Speaker, 37–38, 43, 44, 113
Speaker interviews, knowledge of speaker's topic, 52
Speaker, Message, Audience Cycle (SMAC), Howard, Dr. Sheena, 113
Speaking down to audience, condescending statements, 43
Speaking situation or setting, considerations of, 6
Specific instance, examples, 61
Speech, 24, 64–65, 82, 155, 156
Speech content, definitions, examples, statistics, testimony, 150
Speech delivery, tools of, 24
Speech evidence, placing of, 65–67
Speech goal, support for, 67
Speech organization, 70, 71, 155
Speech practice, 141, 155, 156
Speech preparation, allows focus on audience, 140
Speech presentation with others, split time, 155
Speech rate, 41, 65
Speech structure, 82–83, 150
Speech to get audience to do something, change a procedure, 18
Spoken words, clarity of, 132
Stage fright. *See* Anxiety
Stanton, Andrew, 89, 94
State topic or purpose of speech, 76
Stationery for thank you letter, 210
Statistics, 60, 61, 75, 151, 152
Steps in speech making, 16
Stock Issues Model, 100–102

INDEX

Stories, 39, 41
Strategic ambiguity, definition of, 203
Stress, physiological response to, 137–140
Strongest evidence, at beginning of speech, 67
Structural inherency, 101
Subordination, in outline, 71
Superordination, top main point, 71
Supporting materials to help audience understand, examples, 151
Supportive audience, type of audience, 34
Survey Monkey, 32, 45–48
Surveys, to build engagement in speech, 23
Sympathy, 88, 91
Symposiums, defined, 179
Synchronous communication, 2

Team meetings, 166; *see also* Virtual meetings
Team sales presentation, 15
Technical prep for virtual interview, 197, 198
Technology, 6, 10
Telephone patent, by Alexander Graham Bell, 2
Television, verbal and nonverbal communication, 3
"Tell me about yourself" question, 200
Testimony, 63, 151, 152–153
Text, match company's website, 158
Thank you, 156, 210
Theme, as narrative element of message, 94
Thesis statement for presentation, 150
Thinking brain, re-label and rename, 144–146
Time, 9, 14, 35
Time for questions and answers, in speech organization, 155
Timing of speech, practice, 36, 156
Title slide, 153
Tolerance of dissent, 89, 106
Topic selection, focus on audience and learn about them, 116
Training sessions. *See* Virtual meetings
Transitional phrase, in conclusion, 77
Transitions, in speech delivery, 16
Triune brain, 138
Trump, Donald, campaign of, 38
Truth, Sojourner, 1
Truthfulness, accuracy and honesty, essential to integrity of communication, 105
"Truthiness" defined by Stephen Colbert, 60
Twain, Mark, on the right word, 92
Twentieth century technology boom, 2
Type--large enough to read from back of room, 158

U.S. Copyright Act, fair use guidelines, 112
Understand and respect other communicators, before evaluating their messages, 106
Unethical communication, 105, 108
Upgrade a product, speech to get audience to do something, 19

Verbal communication, effect on audiences, 38–40
Verbal information, definition of, 6
VIA3, for web browser meetings, 167
Video, web camera on or off, 168
Video conferencing platform, 150
Video interview, 195 Also see Online interviewing
Video conferences. *See* Virtual meetings
Videos, practice use of before meeting, 172
Videos online, with text of speech or captioning, 117
Vines, citations required for, 64
Virtual backgrounds, 197
Virtual events, 8, 9
Virtual fatigue, 23
Virtual job interviewing, 196–197, 208, 210
Virtual meetings,165–176
Virtual presentations, 4, 7, 9, 10, 13–27
Virtual presenting, characteristics of, 10
Virtual speaker, set stage for performance, 30
Virtual speech. *See* Online speech
Virtual training meetings, 166
Visual aids, 15, 16, 149-150, 153–157, 160-162
Visual cues, speech delivery tool, 24
Visual design, 159–160
Visualization, 82, 92, 143
Vocal segregates, definition of, 132
Vocal variety, in speech delivery, 16
Vocalics, 3, 40. *See also* Paralanguage
Voice, sets tone in virtual interview, 24, 208–209
Volume and rate of speech, 132
Voluntary audience, audience type, 35

Web-browser meeting platform, 167
Web conferences. *See* Virtual meetings
Web platforms. 168-170
Webex, server-based platforms, 168
Webinars, 166. *See also* Virtual meetings
Wedding speech, occasion or time, 33

Welch, Suzy, on proper attire for workplace, 207
"What are your current salary expectations?" question, 200
"When I'm done with my presentation, I want the audience to know--," 69–70
Whiteboards, 150, 169
"Why do you want to work for us?" question, 201
Wi-Fi Router, close to for online communication, 127
Wikipedia, 55, 57
Wiley, open-access journals, 55
Williams, Kaylene, on fear appeals, 115
Williams, William Carolos, "Red Wheelbarrow," 93
Witte, Kim, fear appeals, 116
Women's Rights Convention, 1
Wonder, for web browser meetings, 167
Words have power, 38–40
World Wide Web, videoconferencing and videotelephony, 3. *See also* Web
Write out presentation, with full sentences, 151

"Yesterday was a day that will live in history." Roosevelt's speech, 2
Yousafzai, Malala, *The Story of the Girl who Stood Up for Education...*, 93
YouTube videos, citations required for, 64

Z-library, free information source, 53
Zoom, for web browser meetings, 167
Zoom breakout rooms, 194
Zoom fatigue, strategies for combatting of, 33